JAEPL, Vol. 26, 2021

JAEPL

The Assembly for Expanded Perspectives on Learning (AEPL), an official assembly of the National Council of Teachers of English, is open to all those interested in extending the frontiers of teaching and learning beyond the traditional disciplines and methodologies.

The purposes of AEPL are to provide a common ground for theorists, researchers, and practitioners to explore innovative ideas; to participate in relevant programs and projects; to integrate these efforts with others in related disciplines; to keep abreast of activities along these lines of inquiry; and to promote scholarship on and publication of these activities.

The *Journal of the Assembly for Expanded Perspectives on Learning, JAEPL,* also provides a forum to encourage research, theory, and classroom practices involving expanded concepts of language. It contributes to a sense of community in which scholars and educators from pre-school through the university exchange points of view and boundary-pushing approaches to teaching and learning. *JAEPL* is especially interested in helping those teachers who experiment with new strategies for learning to share their practices and confirm their validity through publication in professional journals.

Topics of interest include but are not limited to:

- Aesthetic, emotional & moral intelligences
- Learning archetypes
- Kinesthetic knowledge & body wisdom
- Ethic of care in education
- Creativity & innovation
- Pedagogies of healing
- Holistic learning
- Humanistic & transpersonal psychology
- Environmentalism
- (Meta)Cognition

- Imaging & visual thinking
- Intuition & felt sense theory
- Meditation & pedagogical uses of silence
- Narration as knowledge
- Reflective teaching
- Spirituality
- New applications of writing & rhetoric
- Memory & transference
- Multimodality
- Social justice

Membership in AEPL is $45. Contact Sheila Kennedy, AEPL, Membership Chair, email: kennedsh@lewisu.edu. Membership includes current year's issue of *JAEPL*.

Send submissions, address changes, and single hardcopy requests to Wendy Ryden, Editor, *JAEPL*, email: wendy.ryden@liu.edu. Address letters to the editors and all other editorial correspondence to Wendy Ryden (wendy.ryden@liu.edu).

AEPL website: www.aepl.org
Back issues of *JAEPL*: http://trace.tennessee.edu/jaepl/
Blog: https://aeplblog.wordpress.com/
Visit Facebook at **Assembly for Expanded Perspectives on Learning**
Production of *JAEPL* is managed by Parlor Press, www.parlorpress.com.

Assembly for Expanded Perspectives on Learning

Executive Board	
Chair	Bruce Novak, Foundation for Ethics and Meaning
Associate Chair	Nate Mickelson, New York University
Secretary	Bob Lazaroff, Nassau Community College, SUNY
Acting Treasurer	Nate Mickelson, New York University
Ex-officio	Marlowe Miller, University of Massachusetts, Lowell
TRACE Website	Elizabeth DeGeorge, University of Tennessee, Knoxville
AEPL Website	Daniel J. Weinstein, Indiana University of Pennsylvania
Advisory Board	Chair: Peter Elbow, University of Massachusetts, Amherst
	Sheridan Blau, Teachers College, Columbia University
	Alice G. Brand, SUNY College at Brockport
	John Creger, American High School, Freemont, CA
	Richard L. Graves, Auburn University, Emeritus
	Doug Hesse, University of Denver
	Nel Noddings, Stanford University
	Sondra Perl, Lehman College, CUNY
	Kurt Spellmeyer, Rutgers University
	Charles Suhor, NCTE
	Peter Stillman, Charlotteville, NY
	Jane Tompkins, University of Illinois at Chicago
	Robert Yagelski, SUNY Albany
Founding Members	Alice G. Brand, SUNY College at Brockport
	Richard L. Graves, Auburn University, Emeritus
	Charles Suhor, NCTE
Membership Contact	Sheila M. Kennedy, Lewis University
JAEPL Editor	Wendy Ryden, Long Island University

JAEPL is a non-profit journal published yearly by the Assembly for Expanded Perspectives on Learning with support from TRACE at University of Tennessee, Knoxville. Back issues are archived at: http://trace.tennessee.edu/jaepl/.

JAEPL gratefully acknowledges this support as well as that of its manuscript reviewers:

Caleb Corkery, Millersville University of Pennsylvania
Resa Crane Bizzaro
Peggy F. Hopper, Mississippi State University
Brandi Lawless, University of San Francisco
Keith Lloyd, Kent State University Stark
Laurence Musgrove, Angelo State University
Jeffrey Ringer, University of Tennessee, Knoxville
Anna Sicari, Oklahoma State University
Joonna Trapp, Emory University
Christy Wenger, Shepherd University
Jeffrey Wilhelm, Boise State University

JAEPL

The Journal of the Assembly for Expanded Perspectives on Learning

Editor
Wendy Ryden
Long Island University

Book Review Editor
Irene Papoulis
Trinity College

"Connecting" Editor
Christy Wenger
Shepherd University

Copyright © 2021
by the Assembly for Expanded Perspectives on Learning
All rights reserved

(ISSN 1085-4630)

An affiliate of the National Council of Teachers of English
Member of the NCTE Information Exchange Agreement
Member of the Council of Editors of Learned Journals
Indexed with MLA Bibliography
Website: www.aepl.org
Blog: https://aeplblog.wordpress.com/
Visit Facebook at **Assembly for Expanded Perspectives on Learning**
Back issues available at: http://trace.tennessee.edu/jaepl/

Volume 26 • 2021

Contents

Special Section
Locations of Spirituality—
Finding Identities; Finding Common Ground

Wendy Ryden	1	Introduction: Losing My Religion
Michael-John DePalma	4	Fostering Ethical Engagement Across Religious Difference in the Context of Rhetorical Education
Kevin Roozen	23	Acting with Inscriptions: Expanding Perspectives of Writing, Learning, and Becoming
Christopher Basgier	49	Contemplative Correspondence and the Muscle of Metaphor: An Interview with Rev. Karen Hering
Christopher Sean Harris and Jorge Ribeiro	62	Winning Hearts, Not Arguments: An Interview with Father Greg Boyle

Essays

Pamela Hartman, Jessica Berg, Hannah Fulton, and Brandon Schuler	66	Memes as Means: Using Popular Culture to Enhance the Study of Literature
Denise Goldman	83	"The Hidden Door That Leads to Several Moments More": Finding Context for the Literacy Narrative in First Year Writing

Connecting

Christy I. Wenger	99	Responding Together and the Roots of Resilience
Sarah Heidebrink-Bruno	103	Reflections from a Working Class, First-Generation Almost-Graduate
Ellen Scheible	107	Collaborative Writing for Publication in Undergraduate Literature Seminars
Naomi Gades	112	(Emily 479)
Paul M. Puccio	113	tra/versing the year

Book Reviews

Irene Papoulis	114	Inserting Oneself in the Story: Queer Literacy, Comics, and an Admonition to Move
Nicholas Marino	114	McBeth, Mark. *Queer Literacies: Discourses and Discontents*
Wilma Romatz	118	Ferris, Emil. *My Favorite Thing Is Monsters* Sousanis, Nick. *Unflattening*

Helen Papoulis	124	Tharp, Twyla. *Keep It Moving: Lessons for the Rest of Your Life*
	127	**Contributors to JAEPL, Vol. 26**

SPECIAL SECTION: LOCATIONS OF SPIRITUALITY—FINDING IDENTITIES; FINDING COMMON GROUND

Introduction: Losing My Religion

Wendy Ryden

This special section, I must confess (pun intended), is by accident, not design (unless you are someone who believes there are no accidents). As the contributions for this year's issue began to coalesce, I saw a pattern emerging in which so much of the work, either directly or indirectly, is steeped in human spirituality as being fundamental to our existences. This fortuitously created an opportunity for organizing the pieces, so I took advantage of that to offer readers this categorical grouping. I am thrilled by the work and the insights these individual contributions provide, and yet I found myself somewhat uneasy assembling them under this banner. AEPL has long recognized spirituality as part of our expanded perspectives on learning, and yet I wondered what it means for an academic journal to focus on this topic—and for me as the editor to facilitate such an emphasis. I decided to devote this brief introduction to an exploration of those nagging feelings of uncertainty by considering, as our authors explicitly and implicitly ask us to do, my own identity, attitudes, and relationship with the spiritual, especially in conjunction with my academic and professional sense of self.

I begin by telling you that I am an apostate. I was raised as a Lutheran (ALC) but currently follow no organized religious practice. My father inherited his religion from his Scandinavian parents, and my mother converted from Catholicism when she married my father (although when times were tough, she always reverted to praying to that Great Mother goddess Mary. Apparently, mom did not see any contradiction.) As a child, I enjoyed (usually) going to Sunday school—the ritual of church not so much. I liked to read Bible stories and learn the history of the Reformation. I was confirmed in the Lutheran church, served as an acolyte, even taught Sunday school. As I grew older, I simply went a different way. The parting was mostly amicable, with some minor existential crises here and there, generally around issues of sexuality.

Today, I am, I suppose, something of a cultural Christian, but my sense of spirituality is fluid, residing somewhere in the camp of eclectic pagan. As an environmentalist, I "commune with nature," something my father used to say when asked about his conspicuous avoidance of church except for Christmas and Easter. I still love Luther's "This is My Father's World" with its celebration of the natural world and devilish hint of animism (phooey on the patriarchal title). I celebrate Christmas with lots of evergreen boughs, and I love the sacred music and art of Europe inspired by the Christian tradition. I also have an abiding interest in learning about other traditions, especially the myths (by which I mean sacred texts, oral and written) that undergird those belief systems and histories.

The problems associated with religion's role in society are legion, ranging from supplanting science and evidence-based inquiry with supernaturalism to justifying and enabling ethno/genocide and gender oppression, to name some highlights. Despite the redemptive and sustaining ways religion has existed in some communities, such as the

African American tradition of Christianity where the church has been an integral part of the struggle for emancipation and equality, it's certainly not hard to see why many folks reject religious belief, both on social and individual levels, to embrace atheism/agnosticism. I often count myself among that group. Religious identification as metonymic displacement for racism, oppression, imperialism, and political struggle are perhaps as old as religion itself, but we are made aware of this phenomenon again and again in the contemporary world, in which we see sizable, seemingly insurmountable rifts forming among us. On the American political scene, the so-called religious right, evangelical nationalism, Opus Dei, among others, have acquired increasing influence over the affairs of state and our daily lives, raising the specter of theocracy in our troubled times. For many of us, faith or no, these prospects are simply horrifying.

Like it (some do) or not (some don't), this is where we are, as the saying goes. We are not operating in an exclusively secular society, and religious beliefs or lack thereof are profound shapers of our identities, both past and present, and mediators of our social existences. Many of us are familiar with the religious student who resists our instructional efforts because they see a conflict between the University's humanism and their own faith-inspired ontology. But I have found the reverse also to be true where students vehemently reject anything that smacks of what they recognize as religion. For these students, sacred texts have been so stigmatized that reading Genesis, for example, means betraying their commitment to a rational order. "I believe in science," a hostile student told me in a world literature class (and I note the irony of expressing what is ostensibly an objective reality in terms of "belief"), as she explained her disinterest in the Hebrew story of creation. The poetry, the philosophy, the cultural and historical impact, for better or worse, were off limits to her as objects of study because the story for her was inseparable from a dogma and religiosity she found abhorrent. Religion or what is perceived as such, whether one professes faith or not, seems to be, like politics, a taboo subject for some students, as though separation of church and state requires public silence about it altogether. In many ways, this makes sense as a measure to protect First Amendment privacy. But religious identities and orientations are not simply private matters. They are often potent public forces that require our reckoning both in our work with students and with ourselves.

The essays and interviews that follow here differ in focus and intent and offer us many ideas and insights about multiple topics and issues, not only spirituality. But they share nonetheless an intrepidity that takes us beyond the anemic realm of tolerance and diversity and other multicultural appropriations from politically correct culture as they ask us to investigate our spiritual orientations in the way we think about ourselves and the way we think about each other. What role do these aspects of our lives play in our reading, writing, teaching, learning—our being and our becoming? The work in this section asks us to be generous in our outlook and open to new ways of experiencing the spiritual dimension of our existences, our mindful practices, our relations with others. What does it mean to take these aspects of people's lives seriously and with the intent to truly understand? Can we bring a liberal, inclusive yet critical relativism to bear productively on our differences to find commonalities or to allow our beliefs to change, evolve? Can we avoid the toxic morass of siloism and group-think that repels us from one another to engage, without unacceptable sacrifice, with this very human dimension of our existences?

The work in this section invites, perhaps even insists, that we do so, that we embrace our senses of being and spirituality with *capaciousness*, to use the term of our essayists, as we take stock of the effects of our own attitudes, beliefs, practices and those of others.

Fostering Ethical Engagement Across Religious Difference in the Context of Rhetorical Education

Michael-John DePalma

Abstract: *At a moment in which religious diversity is ever-increasing in the United States and more than three-quarters of the world's population identifies with a religious tradition, it is important for writing teachers to consider how to best cultivate writers who are equipped to build identifications across religious difference. This essay traces my efforts to engage this exigence in my advanced undergraduate writing course at Baylor University entitled Religious Rhetorics and Spiritual Writing (RRSW). In what follows, I outline my pedagogical goals, course design, and approach to teaching RRSW. I then share the results of a qualitative pilot study that used teacher-research methodology to develop an understanding of what students learned about engaging across religious difference in RRSW. Results of this study show that students learned the value of approaching rhetorical engagement across religious difference with dispositions of hospitality, curiosity, and humility. Specifically, they came to see 1) the importance of using language that is grounded in writers' personal histories and accessible to (religiously) diverse audiences; 2) the value of approaching religious and spiritual writing as a process of inquiry; and 3) the significance of holding capacious notions of religious and spiritual rhetorics. After discussing the implications of students' learning in RRSW, I conclude the essay by articulating ways that more intentional engagement with scholarship in interfaith studies can assist teachers of writing in our efforts to enrich writers' capacities to engage with religious difference in productive ways.*

> "Our sacred traditions should help us live more thoughtfully, generously, and hopefully with the tensions of our age. But to grasp that, we must look anew at the very nature of faith, and at what it might really mean to take religion seriously in human life and in the world."
>
> —Krista Tippett, *Speaking of Faith: Why Religion Matters—and How to Talk about It*

> "We must treat one another with empathy, attentiveness, and trust; we must take the time to invent and continually reinvent our ideas in the light of informed disagreement; we must care enough about our own views to try to persuade others of them, but not so much that we are unwilling to change them; we must listen with care to people who tell us we are wrong; we must behave with grace when other views prevail; we must argue with passion but without rancor, with commitment but without intransigence."
>
> —Patricia Roberts-Miller, *Deliberate Conflict: Argument, Political Theory, and Composition Classes*

Scholars in rhetoric and writing studies have long been committed to discovering how we might best equip rhetors to engage across difference in ways that promote understanding, connection, and empathy while also allowing space for dissonance and disagreement (see, for example, Baca, et al.; Bizzell and Herzberg; Blankenship; Canagarajah; Hum and Lyon; Pratt; Ratcliffe; Trimbur). Conceptions of rhetoric that have for decades remained vital to the work of the field reflect enduring concerns about how to productively negotiate difference. Wayne Booth, for example, offers his notion of "rhetorology" as a form of "listening rhetoric" that seeks to "reduc[e] misunderstanding by paying full attention to opposing views" (10). Rhetorology, Booth hopes, "teaches that learning to listen, and encouraging our opponents to listen, can *sometimes* yield moments of sheer illumination: a trustful pursuit of truth replacing what had appeared to be a hopeless battle" (172). Kenneth Burke conceptualizes rhetoric as a symbolic means of inducing cooperation among interlocuters who are "both joined and separate, at once a distinct substance and consubstantial with another" (21). Efforts to traverse our divisions and achieve consubstantiality, he argues, necessitate identification. Sonja J. Foss and Cindy L. Griffin, too, theorize invitational rhetoric as "an invitation to understanding as a means to create a relationship rooted in equality, immanent value, and self-determination." In the midst of our ongoing encounters with a diversity of perspectives, invitational rhetoric is offered as a framework for interaction that seeks for rhetors and audiences to gain "understanding that engenders appreciation, value, and a sense of equity" (5).

Exigent questions concerning how best to foster the kinds of writing knowledge, abilities, and dispositions that are essential for thoughtful engagement across difference in our twenty-first century context have likewise influenced current approaches to rhetorical education in generative ways (see, for instance, Clifton; Duffy; Glenn et al.; Roberts-Miller). Scholarship in this vein offers valuable pedagogical insights concerning ways to prepare writers to engage in ethical deliberation. A dimension of difference that we have yet to adequately account for in our discussions of twenty-first century rhetorical education, however, is engagement across religious difference.

Religious diversity is a major facet of our contemporary context in the United States and around the world. Sociologists of religion widely assert that the United States is more religiously diverse in our present moment than in any other previous era in recorded history (Jones and Cox 10). On a global scale, there are equally dramatic shifts in religious affiliation underway that are altering the world's religious landscape. Not only is this ever-increasing diversity of the world's religious composition significant to the more than 84 percent of the world's population who identify as religiously affiliated (Pew Forum on Religion and Public Life, "Global" 9) or the more than 75 percent of Americans who claim religious affiliation (Pew Forum on Religion and Public Life, "Religious"), but these shifting dynamics pertain to all who are concerned with how to promote peaceful, respectful, and ethical forms of engagement across difference in our present moment. Readers are all too familiar with the long record of tragedies in which clashes over religious difference have fueled wars, genocide, oppression, demagoguery, violent hate crimes, harassment, and other such ills. These religious conflicts erode human dignity, sever bonds, undermine deliberation, and threaten the very foundations of democracy. Such outcomes, however, are in no way a given and indeed may be subject to intervention through rhetorical education.

Interfaith scholars and activists have shown that it is possible to proactively engage with religious difference in ways that foster mutual respect, collaboration, and a shared commitment to promoting peace (see, for example, Patel, *Interfaith*). Constructive engagement across religious difference, however, first requires recognition that "the vibrancy of civic life is enhanced by religious participation and … religious diversity in its broadest sense" (Lewis and Cantor xiii). Relatedly, it demands a commitment to teaching citizens knowledge, skills, and dispositions for engaging religious diversity toward positive ends (e.g., social connectedness, civic cooperation, human flourishing). The decision to pursue such a commitment is highly consequential at this juncture. As Earl Lewis and Nancy Cantor rightly note in *Out of Many Faiths: Religious Diversity and The American Promise*, "there is every reason to wonder whether the American democratic project, built on a promise of religious diversity and freedom amid a reality of expectations of assimilation, can stretch and evolve sufficiently to reap the benefits of the insights and talents of new communities of faith in our midst" (xiv). As a discipline that is committed to educating communicators for thoughtful public deliberation in our twenty-first century context, rhetoric and writing studies is well-equipped to contribute in important ways to the pursuit of this American democratic project. Our ability to do so, however, requires that we give increased attention to preparing writers to engage with the plurality of religious orientations in productive ways. Specifically, we must consider how best to foster the kinds of knowledge, abilities, and dispositions that writers need to build identifications across religious difference in the context of rhetorical education.

This essay traces my efforts to engage this exigence in my advanced undergraduate writing course at Baylor University entitled Religious Rhetorics and Spiritual Writing (RRSW). In what follows, I outline my pedagogical goals, course design, and approach to teaching RRSW. I then share the results of a qualitative pilot study that used teacher-research methodology to develop an understanding of what students learned about engaging across religious difference in RRSW. Results of this study show that students in RRSW learned the rhetorical value of approaching religious difference with dispositions of hospitality, curiosity, and humility. Specifically, they came to see 1) the importance of using language that is grounded in writers' personal histories and accessible to (religiously) diverse audiences; 2) the value of approaching religious and spiritual writing as a process of inquiry; and 3) the significance of holding capacious notions of religious and spiritual rhetorics. After discussing the implications of students' learning in RRSW, I conclude the essay by articulating ways that more intentional engagement with scholarship in interfaith studies can assist teachers of writing in our efforts to enrich writers' capacities to engage with religious difference in constructive ways.

Teaching Religious Rhetorics and Spiritual Writing: Context, Motives, and Pedagogy

Religious Rhetorics and Spiritual Writing (RRSW) is a course I designed and teach regularly. Baylor is the largest private, Baptist university in the world with a total of 18,033 undergraduate and graduate students as of Spring 2020. Baylor students come from all 50 states and 91 foreign countries ("Profile"). In Fall 2019, nearly 90 percent of Baylor undergraduates identified with some denomination of Christianity ("Profile"). Of the 36 different Christian affiliations reported, the largest number of students identified as Baptist (24.7 percent), Christian, no affiliation (19.6 percent), Catholic (16.9 percent), and non-denominational (8.2 percent). Among the 10 percent of Baylor undergraduates who did not identify as Christian, students reported religious affiliations with Buddhism (.5 percent), Hinduism (1.1 percent), Judaism (.1 percent), and Islam (.8 percent). Among that 10 percent of students were also undergraduates who claimed no religious affiliation (4.8 percent) and students who identified as atheists (.5 percent). Although Baylor is historically Baptist, students who attend Baylor do not sign a statement of faith as is the case at some other religiously affiliated colleges and universities. It is true that there are many students for whom the university's religious identity is a draw, but this is not true for all. It is also important to note that even though a majority of students at Baylor identify with some form of Christianity, there is a diverse spectrum of intra-religious differences, identities, and ways of being represented within that overarching category.

The mission of Baylor University is to "educate men and women for worldwide leadership and service by integrating academic excellence and Christian commitment in a caring community" ("Mission Statement"). Given the diversity of the global religious landscape, I have come to see the cultivation of writers who are prepared to engage positively with religious diversity as an essential dimension of fulfilling this mission. Educating students for worldwide leadership and service demands a rhetorical education that trains all students—whether they are devoted religious followers, "culturally religious," or atheists—to engage religious diversity in ethical and productive ways. I believe this to be true not only for Baylor University but for any institution (religiously affiliated or not) that seeks to prepare global leaders to navigate the rhetorical complexities of communicating across interreligious and intrareligious differences as well as agnostic and atheistic perspectives in our religiously pluralistic democracy.

In seeking how to best prepare communicators for generative engagement across religious difference, John Duffy's scholarship on rhetorical virtues and the relational nature of writing proves foundational and indispensable. In "The Good Writer: Virtue Ethics and the Teaching of Writing," Duffy insightfully argues that "writing involves ethical decisions because every time we write ... we propose a relationship with others, our readers" (229). In linking rhetorical practices to ethical choices, Duffy encourages teachers of writing to contemplate how our writing pedagogies might encourage writers to enact the kinds of ethical dispositions and rhetorical virtues that we seek to nurture through rhetorical education. Ethical dispositions, Duffy explains, include writers' "tendencies, habits, and practices, such as fair-mindedness, tolerance, judgment, intellectual courage, that speak to the character of an individual ... and are enacted in the course of reading and composing texts" ("Ethical" 219). Closely linked to ethical dispositions are rhetorical virtues, which Duffy defines as "the discursive practices of virtue, the expression in speech and writing of honesty, accountability, generosity, and other qualities"—qualities that "reflect the traits, attitudes, and dispositions we associate with a good person, speaking or writing well" ("Ethical" 235). The notion that writing necessarily requires writers to make ethical choices that have significant consequences, both in terms of writers' ethical formation and in terms of their relationships with readers, profoundly shaped the ways writers in RRSW were invited to engage with religious differences. Specifically, it meant framing all of the writing that students would take up in RRSW as relational work. In doing so, I aimed to encourage habits of mind that would enable writers to engage productively and ethically with intra-, inter-, and non-religious difference.

Scholarship in the fields of religion and interfaith studies on the value of narrative and nonfiction storytelling also significantly animated the design of the writing projects that students took up in RRSW. In *The One and the Many: America's Struggle for the Common Good*, Martin E. Marty, world-renowned religion scholar, argues "The narratives and myths of each group ... must be allowed to be told and heard across boundaries and in all sectors. Only then can the virtues and values that people claim for these stories be tested. Only thus can they flow in various directions within the separate groups and between any of them and the society at large" (10). Narratives crafted, shared, and contemplated across intra/interreligious perspectives, Marty asserts, offer possibilities for engagement across difference that might otherwise be unavailable in a discursive climate characterized by turbulent, hostile, and toxic discourse. In *Interfaith Leadership: A Primer*, interfaith scholar and activist Eboo Patel likewise attests to the power of crafting narratives that allow writers to articulate the shifting dynamics of their identities and forge connections with readers who orient differently around religion. The critical role of narrative as a rhetorical resource for negotiating religious difference undergirded all of the major writing projects that writers completed in RRSW. In particular, each project offered an opportunity for writers to create narratives that would allow them to come to terms with their motives, values, and beliefs. The awareness gained by making these tacit dimensions of their thinking explicit created a basis upon which writers could then begin to consider how they might build identification across difference. In naming, unraveling, and challenging their motives, values, and beliefs through their narratives, writers were offered occasions to reflect on, reimagine, or remake relationships.

Recent work on religion and the teaching of writing was also particularly helpful in imagining how best to prepare writers to navigate our religiously pluralistic twenty-first century context. Based on conversations with colleagues at a range of institutions, I surmise that there is a strong and growing interest in rhetorical education centered on engagement with religious rhetorics. I am aware of a number of excellent courses being taught across the United States, and I am sure that there are more still undiscovered. However, there remains a dearth of published scholarship that engages with religious rhetorics in the context of rhetorical education. I am grateful, though, for the notable exceptions that have informed my pedagogy in formative ways. These include courses taught by Chris S. Earle at the University of Nevada, Reno (see Earle), undergraduate courses taught by TJ Geiger at Syracuse University (see Geiger), and graduate and undergraduate courses taught by Jeff Ringer at the University of Tennessee (see Ringer, "Dogma"). A central focus of this scholarship concerns possibilities for teaching writers to engage religious diversity in thoughtful and productive ways (see also DePalma, "Reimagining"; Ringer, *Vernacular*; Williams). These writing specialists view the ability to engage rhetorically across religious difference as an essential civic capacity, and several of these scholars suggest that teaching writers to construct narratives centered on (religious) values (Ringer, *Vernacular*), identities (Geiger), beliefs (DePalma, "Re-envisioning"), and literacies (Williams) in relation to writers' human contexts can serve as a vital basis for rhetorical engagement across religious difference. It is these lines of thinking that led me to design RRSW.

RRSW is centered on producing narratives to enable thoughtful and ethical engagement with differing religious perspectives. In this course, students compose a variety of work—spiritual autobiographies, religious literacy essays, histories of belief, epideictic discourses, and other related genres—to gain expertise writing from experience and critically analyzing the perspectives they encounter. Through these genres, writers explore spiritual questions, religious issues, and rhetorical concerns in order to articulate, reflect on, and reconsider their beliefs and values in relation to other students and authors. For my students, opportunities to engage through writing with religious beliefs and values are rare in academic settings and in their (religious) communities. Thus, in creating a space where writers can craft such nonfiction narratives, I aim to facilitate moments of discovery, dissonance, and dialogue that will better enable writers to respectfully and ethically engage with a diversity of beliefs and values in and beyond the course. With these aims in mind, writers in RRSW take up three major writing projects, craft several weekly writing assignments, and deliver three formal presentations.

The three major writing projects are "This I Believe Audio Essay," "Epideictic Essay and Speech," and "Multimodal Spiritual Autobiography." For the "This I Believe" project, students articulate a sacred belief in relation to a particular moment, event, or experience that has been essential in shaping, testing, or illuminating that belief. The goal is for students to craft a compelling narrative that conveys a belief they live by in a manner that is accessible to an audience who does not share the belief. Students are instructed to convey not only what they believe but how they reached their beliefs. They are also encouraged to take their beliefs out of the ether and ground them in the events of their lives through a story that embodies the essence of the belief. This guidance is essential for helping writers develop awareness about how they might best convey their beliefs to audiences who may not share them. The texts students read in preparing to compose their "This I Believe Audio Essay" are drawn primarily from the collections *This I Believe I* and *This I Believe II* (Allison and Gediman). They also read essays by writers such as Langston Hughes, Jo Ann Beard, and Annie Dillard and listen to several audio essays.

In the "Epideictic" assignment, students make manifest an unnoticed or invisible virtue of a person they know, have known, or know about by commemorating an admirable quality or virtuous action of that individual. Here students attempt to invent language that makes visible the extraordinary in human experience and to write narrative profiles of figures who exemplify the virtue articulated. Students are instructed that their primary goal is to encourage audience acknowledgment or appreciation, especially among those members of the audience who may not value what is praised. In writing a tribute that attempts to bind the speaker and the audience together as members of a community, writers are encouraged to use words and images that make the person and his or her qualities present to the audience. Students are instructed to use concrete, precise, and clear language so the audience can imagine the person's qualities through specific actions, words, or ideas. To prepare for the project, students read Lawrence Prelli's *Rhetorics of Display* and Sharon Crowley and Deborah Hawhee's *Ancient Rhetorics for Contemporary Students*, profiles from *The New Yorker* and *The Atlantic*, and excerpts from David Brooks's *The Road to Character*. They also view and analyze a range of TED talks to discern conventions of effective delivery for their tributes.

For the "Spiritual Autobiography" project, students compose a narrative that examines the sacred mysteries, broader truths, or spiritual experiences that have shaped their engagement with ultimate questions. The purpose of this project is to provide writers the opportunity to explore a sacred dimension of their life experience in a way that is accessible, significant, and interesting to readers who may not share the writer's beliefs, values, or experiences. They also try to develop a new perspective on the experience and their beliefs and values. Students are reminded to resist the inclination to work from a predetermined thesis and instead allow the process of composing to reveal insight into the writer's questions as the essay unfolds. They are also assured at the outset and throughout the project that their spiritual autobiographies will not likely follow a straight narrative line but will proceed more intuitively, meandering from point to point in a way that actually forms a path toward insight in retrospect. By asking students to engage with their lived experience in this way, I invite them to see the complexity of sacred beliefs, values, and experiences—insights which can lead to greater sensitivity, empathy, and respect when engaging with their own or others', especially dissimilar, beliefs and values. In order to provide writers with a range of effective approaches in this expansive and diverse genre, we read several essays from *The Best Spiritual Writing* series, Amy Mandelker and Elizabeth Powers' *Pilgrim Souls: A Collection of Spiritual Autobiographies*, and Elizabeth J. Andrews' *Writing the Sacred Journey: The Art and Practice of Spiritual Memoir*. Some of the writers we read in this unit include Andre Dubus, Scott Russell Sanders, David James Duncan, Pico Iyer, and Brenda Miller. Finally, writers view and analyze several digital stories in preparation for their own multimodal spiritual autobiographies.

Taken together, the primary objective of all three projects is to help students develop the narrative resources needed to articulate their guiding (religious) beliefs and values in relation to their human context and lived experiences in ways that are accessible to (religiously) diverse audiences. A key assumption animating these projects is that it is essential for writers to reflect on and explain their own deeply held motives, values, and beliefs in order to build identification with readers whose motives, values, and beliefs differ from their own. In learning to more thoughtfully share their beliefs and values through nonfiction narratives with audiences of different perspectives, students can develop renewed understanding of their own traditions and communities and learn to appreciate other traditions as well. Since students are required to present their three major writing projects to audiences beyond our immediate class (e.g., members of the local community, members of the wider university community, National Public Radio listeners), they are very conscious of working to craft their pieces for diverse audiences.

Initial Research Findings

During the sixteen-week semester that I first taught RRSW, I conducted a qualitative pilot study that used teacher-research methodology, a fitting approach to understand students' learning as they wrote narratives engaged with religious perspectives. This IRB-approved study was guided by the following question: What are the learning outcomes of writing instruction that positions writers to use narrative as a means of articulating their (religious) values and beliefs to (religiously) diverse audiences? The data collected for this study included (a) course documents, including the course syllabus, project assignment sheets, assessment rubrics, project guidelines, and course objectives; (b) students' written essays, presentation materials (i.e., audio essays, visual tributes, and multimodal spiritual autobiographies), and written reflections; (c) individual, hour-long, transcribed interviews with all eight members of the class, focused on students' experiences writing from and critically analyzing faith-based and interfaith perspectives; (d) and an hour-long focus group interview with seven of the eight members of the class. Grounded theory guided my approach to data analysis. I began by transcribing the eight digitally recorded interviews and the focus group interview. I then read the interview transcripts alongside students' written projects, presentation materials, and reflection essays to code themes across sources. As a result, a number of themes and sub-themes emerged. As new themes materialized, the codes were continually expanded.

All eight students who were enrolled in my RRSW course participated in this qualitative pilot study.[1] Seven of the students were female, and one was male. Seven of the participants were professional writing and rhetoric majors, and one was an interdisciplinary studies major. Three of the participants were seniors, four were juniors, and one was a sophomore. One participant identified as Asian-American, one as biracial (white and African American), one as Latinx, and the other five as white. One of the participants identified as "Christian, protestant, evangelical," another as Reformed Baptist, another as "spiritual but not religious," and the other five participants as "nondenominational Christian."

Results of this study show that students learned the value of approaching rhetorical engagement across religious difference with dispositions of hospitality, curiosity, and humility. Specifically, they came to see 1) the importance of using language that is grounded in writers' personal histories and accessible to (religiously) diverse audiences; 2) the value of approaching religious and spiritual writing as a process of inquiry; and 3) the significance of holding capacious notions of religious and spiritual rhetorics.

While the formation of dispositions, knowledge, and capacities needed to navigate the complexities of communication across religious difference require years to take shape, instruction geared toward engagement with religious rhetorics can open possibilities for their initial development. Given that only one class of students participated in this pilot study over a single semester, the findings presented below are offered as preliminary and with the understanding that further research is needed.

Extending Hospitality by Crafting Accessible Narratives of Lived Experience

A key learning outcome for writers in RRSW is that they recognized the value of approaching religious difference through a disposition of hospitality. Extending hospitality meant seeing writing as a relational practice and making intentional changes to routine ways of using language to allow readers to dwell in conversation with them. Writers achieved this posture of intentional hospitality through accessible and concrete writing, grounded in their personal histories. In speaking to the value of accessible nar-

---

1. All students who participated in this IRB-approved study signed written permission forms and were given pseudonyms.

ratives of lived experience, several students emphasized that rhetorical hospitality makes possible identification with readers, many of whom are likely to be unfamiliar with the language of the writer's particular religious tradition. Cecilia, for example, indicated: "We have a lot of lofty terms that we use to describe things that we think are really key to our faith, but they tend to fall flat." In order to avoid this pitfall, Cecilia altered her language practices by "getting away from Christian clichés" and being "more intentional with words." Elaborating on the ways studying and using religious rhetorics has influenced her rhetorical practice, Cecilia remarked,

> I learned this semester that you have to be very careful with words even if you mean them. ... You need to be aware of all of the different things that inform the words and their connotations. And if there is a way [a word] can be interpreted differently, you need to either address that or define it in your own way in the text itself, so that your reader knows what you're talking about.

Cecilia's remarks here indicate an awareness about the consequences of language use and the potential for misunderstanding when engaging across religious difference. She is cognizant that the meanings of terminologies are not static or transparent. She understands that interpretations in these contexts, like all forms of symbolic action, are fluid and negotiated by writers and readers.

This awareness led Cecilia to use "spiritual language that is embodied" when conveying her beliefs to both those who share her faith commitments and those who do not. When asked what she meant by "embodied," she explained that she was referring to language that is grounded in writers' personal experiences and anchored in writers' particular contexts. Cecilia views the use of embodied religious rhetorics as a way of extending hospitality by inviting readers into writers' histories, experiences, and logics. She explains that such language practices help readers understand the ways writers come to their religious beliefs. Language of this kind provides a history and a context for the belief that can foster empathy in the reader. In reflecting on the importance of embodied rhetorics when addressing those who do not share a writer's religious commitments, she states:

> It's kind of amazing to me to think about how there can be so many different ways of approaching spirituality.... So maybe that's why I keep coming back to the term "embodied writing," because you can say like "salvation" to someone and we would all kind of have different memories of books we read or images we've seen attached to that word. We can all believe the same kind of general thing about it, but it would be manifest in very different ways.

An example of the ways Cecilia's insights translated into her work as a writer is a study that she initiated in RRSW and then continued over a two-year period following the course. The project maps historical, literary, theological, biblical, and cultural representations of dance as an embodied sacred art across religions, cultures, and centuries. The study skillfully weaves together Cecilia's rigorous analysis of historical, spiritual, and literary texts with pieces of memoir and literary journalism in order to invite readers into the contours of this conversation.

Students also came to value extending hospitality through the use of accessible language when engaging across religious difference because they recognized its potential for complicating readers' negative perceptions of people who identify as religiously committed. Daniel, for example, explained, "I think in terms of spiritual writing, the more subtle someone can get ... would really benefit their ability to reach a broader audience." He sees the subtlety of such language as a way to "bridge a gap" because it might enable the reader and writer to find points of intersection that are obscured by explicitly religious terminologies and theologically loaded arguments. It is not that the writer is attempting to hide his or her religious identity and commitments but is rather attempting to invent artistic and nuanced ways of conveying his or her beliefs to induce others to hear and consider them. To illustrate what this might look like in practice, Daniel discussed examples of creative strategies that he saw as effective from our course reading: "There were writers who like in *This I Believe* would list a Scripture verse or something, and it was like, 'That's a Christian verse from the Bible,' but the rest of the piece they're not saying anything about God, so it's like you know this person's a Christian, but they don't actually ever say like, 'I believe in Jesus or something.'" Another strategy he mentioned is when writers quote something Jesus said without attributing the statement to him. Other invention strategies he noted were including dream and vision sequences, using biblical imagery and metaphors, and allowing voices other than the essayist's own voice to express particular beliefs. Rhetorical practices of this kind are effective, he explained, because though there are "Christian undertones," such language "is not preachy. It's more subtle. It's not expressly stated." Daniel concluded by stating, "Anyone who wants to affect someone seriously, especially on a spiritual level, has to put serious consideration into the ways they rhetorically frame things." Daniel himself enacted these strategies skillfully in a *This I Believe* essay entitled "I Believe in Microscopes" and a lyric essay entitled "Ichthyology"—two pieces in which he used allegory, poetry, vivid imagery, and personal anecdotes to provoke meditation on intersections of spiritual and scientific inquiry.

Rhetorical hospitality has the potential to facilitate connections among communicators who orient differently around religion. Rather than relying primarily on theological terms or doctrinal statements to communicate their beliefs—rhetorical approaches that build community cohesion but often function as barriers to engagement *across* religious difference—Cecilia and Daniel tried to employ language rooted in their personal experiences and backgrounds. Cecilia, Daniel, and several other students came to see that means readily used to express religious commitments (e.g., planting verses from sacred texts, using religious terminology, outlining doctrinal or theological tenets explicitly) have the potential to alienate especially those readers outside of their own belief systems. Through their assignments, students learned that when writing is steeped in abstract language from a particular religious tradition, there is little chance for constructing meaningful relationships with readers who are not a part of that discourse community (e.g., audiences who are affiliated with another denomination, religion, or no religion at all). They discovered that the nuances and depth of their beliefs are lost on readers when writers rely heavily on stock religious terminology from the writer's own religious tradition. Students thus learned that a hospitable approach requires creating entry points for readers that allow them to consider sacred beliefs or traditions not their own.

Curiosity as a Starting Point for Engaging Religious Rhetorics

A second outcome was understanding the value of approaching religious rhetorics—their own and others—with a disposition of curiosity. While many students initially associated religious rhetorics and spiritual writing with texts that supply answers or argue for particular conclusions, all writers in RRSW came to see the purpose of such language practices as also useful for exploring mysteries, examining ultimate questions, and challenging commonplace ideas. Rather than viewing the purpose of composing religious rhetorics primarily as an effort to convey moral imperatives or persuade readers to adopt a particular set of religious truths—as was the case for several writers when they entered the course—students gained an appreciation for taking up spiritual writing as a means of opening up paths of inquiry about their own religious beliefs and traditions and those of others. For students who were accustomed to religious discourses focused on imparting particular doctrines or values of a tradition, the move to approach such topics from a place of curiosity and as a process of inquiry required a significant shift. This was especially true in cases where students had an understanding of their religious tradition as divinely revealed truth. However, as writers began to engage their deeply held beliefs, values, and commitments in a spirit of genuine curiosity and with a sense of wonder, they came to see the value in exploring concerns they may have taken for granted. They also became more comfortable with the notion that cultivating a disposition of curiosity entails developing patience for uncertainty and ambiguity—qualities which position writers to engage with their own religious traditions and the traditions of others in productive ways.

In reflecting on her gradual movement toward adopting a disposition of curiosity, Cecilia, for example, offers the following:

> There aren't solid answers for a lot of things, and so when you're writing about [religious ideas], I've had to be okay with learning to leave my writing without a lot of real solid conclusions. A lot of the texts that we read ... don't end in a satisfying way, so they seem really raw. ... That is an important aspect of spiritual writing, because no one has all the answers. I think sometimes I have been more influenced by the texts that didn't give me an answer at the end than I would have if they had ended with some imperative about how you should apply this to your life.

Gayle similarly came to see religious rhetorics as guided in large part by questions that do not have concrete or absolute answers: "I think spiritual writing is searching for answers that you know you might not even get. It's just like the questioning. ... Religious writing would be an even more refined version of spiritual writing. Spiritual writing is finding a place among all of it. Religious writing would be finding a place specifically within your own religion or within a specific religion."

Grace also remarked that her writing allowed her to become more comfortable with a disposition of curiosity and using religious rhetorics as a tool for exploring the unknown. She reflected, "I think being comfortable with writing about ideas that I don't understand totally or haven't fully explored and learning to take risks as far as topics and places you go in writing has been valuable. . . . It was the first time I had to think about writing in this way ... approaching things such as the invisible or the ineffable that are very hard to put words to." Grace described the shift this way: "Instead of trying to go through like you have a question and an answer, it's more like, 'Here's the question. Now let's get deeper into this question and think about the question. Even if we don't come to a conclusive answer, that's okay.'" Using writing in these ways, she explained, "is a unique thing to the classes I've taken ... because a lot of it is about coming to a conclusion." In reflecting on her thoughts regarding the value of using writing as a means of exploring religious beliefs and traditions, Grace commented: "It seems like, if it's something you can't express, why are you trying to put words to it? But it is in the process of putting words to it that, even if you can't totally grasp it, there's ... a way of dealing with [these big questions that we all ask] or understanding them better, and that is what spiritual writing can allow you to do."

Cecilia's and Grace's reflections reveal an appreciation for contemplation of enduring and complex questions for which there are no definite answers. While Cecilia and Grace entered RRSW with the assumption that religious rhetorics are forms of communication that aim to impart settled-upon moral truths and life lessons, they eventually came to see the generative power of religious rhetorics and spiritual writing that provoke audiences to meditate on living questions without absolute answers—an understanding that can better position them to engage ethically across religious difference. This disposition of curiosity manifested both in the way writers were willing to challenge themselves to engage with complex open questions and in their conclusions that regularly took the form of invitations for further contemplation rather than summaries of a moral, lesson, or conclusive argument.

Exercising Humility, Expanding Conceptions of Religious Rhetorics, Valuing Spiritual Writing

In addition to fostering hospitality and curiosity, writers also developed a disposition of humility by expanding their notions of religious rhetorics and valuing diverse forms of spiritual writing. At the start of the course, many writers viewed religious rhetorics and spiritual writing as primarily situated within forms of Christianity. The discourses that circulate widely within students' religious communities, the sacred texts they read, and the religious practices they enact all were important influences in shaping their conceptions of "religious rhetorics" or "spiritual writing," giving shape, texture, and grounding to what would otherwise be vague abstractions. The writing students were invited to take up in RRSW, however, enabled them to expand their frames of reference to include religious discourses, texts, and traditions beyond their own. This expansion in their associations with these terminologies led students to recognize that writing can be "spiritual" even if it has no ties to a religious tradition. Such recognition also allowed students to value such writing on its own terms rather than in relation to a particular denomination of Christianity or another form of organized religion—a shift in perspective that not only *required* humility but also led students to see that humility is vital when engaging across religious difference.

Cecilia's reflections illustrate this shift in perspective well. Cecilia initially thought of spiritual writing as "having a very obvious connection to a specific religion." She also tended to think of spiritual writing as being "more evangelistic." The writing she did in RRSW, however, broadened her notions. She explained,

> This class has taught me to think of things as far as spiritual texts from a perspective that wasn't necessarily so deeply tied to Christianity.... The things that we read were very much, I don't want to say in opposition to, but were very different from what you'd find on the shelves of a Christian bookstore. There are a lot of good books that are like that, but I think this class is kind of radical in a way because you see that there is so much writing out there that has the power to actually change people without actually being under the label of Christian nonfiction or something.

Sofia's definitions of religious and spiritual writing were also complicated through our reading and writing. "When I came to the class," she explained, "I was expecting us to read biblical stuff, like people talking about the Bible specifically, and not necessarily their own experiences." After the course, however, Sofia came to believe that "spiritual writing isn't necessarily religious writing. It is about the whole human experience." While she views texts in which "authors talk about God and their spiritual experiences" as spiritual writing, she has come to understand that it "doesn't necessarily need to be connected to religion. It can be about anything, any experience." With regard to the latter, she explained, "I wouldn't have considered that spiritual writing before I came into the class."

Elizabeth discussed a similar shift in her perspective. She explained that prior to taking RRSW, she wouldn't have considered many of the texts we read to be spiritual or religious "because they didn't have anything to do with Christianity." According to her "original definition," her judgments were informed by the following gauge: "It doesn't mention God or Jesus or the Bible so it's not religious or spiritual." As a result of the writing she did in RRSW, however, Elizabeth indicated that she learned to see "how things in everyday life can be spiritual" and "how everyday things can mean something that strongly."

Gayle, too, expressed a shift in her thinking regarding the relationship between religious and spiritual writing: "In the beginning of the semester, I thought of religious writing as the big umbrella and spiritual writing as the little umbrella under it. And so everything spiritual is inversely religious. ... Now, I kind of see spiritual writing as a big umbrella over here and religious writing as a big umbrella kind of a little bit lower, but their edges kind of tip a little bit like a Venn diagram and there is a big area that overlaps, but [spiritual writing] can exist outside by itself." While Gayle initially believed that all spiritual writing is linked to religion in some form or that "there would have to be a certain amount of religious language in spiritual writing," she later came to view spirituality and spiritual writing more broadly. Rather than being necessarily tied to religious thought, she came to see spiritual writing as discourses that explore ontological, existential, epistemological, and metaphysical questions.

Rethinking her ideas about spiritual and religious writing was also an important learning outcome for Grace in RRSW. She indicated that the relationship between religious and spiritual writing "is something [she] thought a lot about throughout the course of the semester." As a result, she came to see spiritual writing as "probing the invisible and putting words to the ineffable." "Spiritual writing," she explained, "isn't necessarily grounded in a certain number of core beliefs or a community of people who believe like you. It is a lot more individualized." It is also concerned with "asking about the significance of things that touch us emotionally or move us." Grace remarked, "You can write about music in a spiritual way and you can write about books in a spiritual way. There are not certain topics that are excluded from spiritual writing. It is the way you're thinking about it. ... There a lot of unanswered questions. Like, 'Here is what I'm wrestling with, and I haven't come to a conclusion yet. Here are my thoughts. Let me give you a peek into what I'm thinking.'"

Cecilia, Sophia, Elizabeth, Gayle, and Grace all came to hold more capacious notions of religious rhetorics and spiritual writing as a result of their writing, conversations, and reading in RRSW. Their conceptions of what constitutes a "religious" or "spiritual" text are not only more expansive, they are also less hierarchical. By experiencing the impact and power of spiritual writing, sacred texts, and religious rhetorics that were not situated within their own religious traditions, students learned to value them on their own terms and, in many respects, on equal footing. Recognizing their value as "religious," "sacred," or "spiritual" texts—categories which previously would have only been extended to their most cherished and holy texts within Christian tradition—students exercised a disposition of humility. In doing so, they were able to engage in relational thinking that troubled the reductive binary between notions of "religious" and "spiritual" and begin to reimagine the relationships among varieties of religious and spiritual experience within and across religious traditions and practices. An example of the way students' expanding notions of spiritual and religious writing emerged in their writing practices is the broad range of subjects that students took up in their efforts to explore their ultimate questions and concerns. For example, students wrote about scars, literacy, food, pens, dance, ghosts, dreams, writing, literature, and a host of other subjects as central to their religious and spiritual formation. As a result of such learning, the writers in RRSW are apt to be better prepared to engage across religious difference.

Potential Implications

In studying and composing religious rhetorics in RRSW, students came to recognize the value of approaching rhetorical engagement across religious difference with dispositions of hospitality, curiosity, and humility. More specifically, students reported that as a result of the writing projects they carried out, they acquired an awareness of the importance of using accessible language that is rooted in their personal experiences and histories when conveying belief across (religious) difference, they started to see religious rhetorics as starting points for inquiry, and they began to think in more expansive ways about the nature and value of religious and spiritual writing. Acquiring these forms of rhetorical awareness is significant in that such awareness can function as a basis for forging common ground and building mutual respect. Students' emerging rhetorical awareness in this regard can encourage them to mobilize the wisdom of their particular traditions to increase appreciation about religious traditions generally. Moreover, the rhetorical awareness that was initiated for writers in RRSW can position them to cultivate connections among citizens and communities who orient differently around religion. Finally, the rhetorical awareness students gained has the potential to serve as a foundation from which these writers can strengthen the cohesion of our religiously diverse democracy and contribute to the making of a more just world.

While additional longitudinal research is required to determine how the rhetorical awareness that students gained will influence them over the long haul, the preliminary findings suggest that writing courses focused on religious rhetorics can function as sites for cultivating writers who have the dispositions, rhetorical knowledge, and capacities to engage religious diversity toward positive ends. The promising indications of these initial findings suggest that it is worthwhile for rhetorical educators to further consider how we might best marshal our expertise in our classrooms to position writers to engage with diverse religious beliefs and values in productive and thoughtful ways.

Extending the Conversation: Cultivating Interfaith Rhetorical Engagement in Twenty-First Century Writing Courses

Throughout this essay, I have argued that attention to religious rhetorics and engagement across religious difference ought to be a primary concern for rhetorical educators who aim to foster dispositions, knowledge, and abilities essential to thoughtful civic engagement in the twenty-first century. My goal in this article has been to initiate a conversation about this exigent line of inquiry, but much future work on rhetorical education and religious rhetorics is required by scholar-teachers in our field to determine how rhetorical educators might best cultivate the kinds of rhetorical awareness, knowledge, and abilities needed to navigate the complexities of our religiously pluralistic democracy. A promising path that researchers in rhetoric and writing studies can pursue is to become better acquainted with the perspectives of scholars in interfaith studies and to utilize their insights in our pedagogies. Thus, in closing my essay, I turn to the insights of Eboo Patel, a compelling voice at the center of the conversation around interfaith engagement, activism, and leadership. Patel is the founder and president of Interfaith Youth Core (IFYC), a nonprofit organization that partners with colleges and universities for the purpose of promoting generative engagement with religious diversity. I believe Patel's ideas concerning interfaith leadership can contribute much to the work of teacher-scholars in rhetoric and writing studies as we seek to prepare writers to engage ethically with religious diversity.

In "Toward a Field of Interfaith Studies," Patel defines an interfaith leader as a citizen "who has the framework, knowledge base, and skill set needed to help individuals and communities who orient around religion differently in civil society and politics build mutual respect, positive relationships, and a commitment to the common good" (40). In *Interfaith Leadership: A Primer*, Patel articulates five potential civic goods of interfaith leadership. They include: 1) enriching understanding of diverse identities and correcting prejudices rooted in the misunderstanding of identities; 2) promoting social cohesion through the inclusion and accommodation of the broadest possible range of citizens; 3) addressing social concerns by drawing together the diversity of knowledge and expertise across (religious) communities and traditions; 4) deepening understanding of identities within religious communities and fostering connections among diverse communities; and 5) crafting narratives that enable identification among diverse citizens who identify with different (religious) traditions and communities (98-99).

In order to equip citizens to enact these civic goods, they need to develop the knowledge and skill set particular to interfaith leadership work. The knowledge base of an interfaith leader, according to Patel, involves developing appreciative knowledge of various religious traditions, a familiarity with theologies of interfaith cooperation, historical awareness of interfaith cooperation during different periods and in a range of contexts, and a sense of shared values that can be used to build cooperative relationships across religious traditions and communities. Relatedly, Patel asserts that the skill set of an interfaith leader entails registering patterns of religious diversity in immediate and wider social contexts and paying attention to the implications of those differences in civic spaces. It also involves learning to mobilize the wisdom and expertise of religiously diverse citizens and communities to address shared problems and initiating community activities that bring together citizens who orient around religion differently. Finally, it enables coordinating conversations about interfaith questions with diverse groups of citizens and inventing public narratives that enable identification across religious difference.

In considering how our expertise in the field of rhetoric and writing studies might contribute to the knowledge base and competencies required for productive interfaith engagement, there are no doubt multiple possibilities. Given the space constraints of this article, however, I will limit my remarks to the final capacity listed above—namely, inventing narratives that enable identification across religious difference. In *Interfaith Leadership*, Patel names three kinds of narratives that are useful for interfaith activists to write: public narratives of interfaith cooperation, binding narratives in religiously diverse communities, and identity narratives that connect personal stories to interfaith work. He also recommends crafting narratives of interactions across religious difference that capture moments of enrichment, connection, conflict, action, and recognition of difference. Drawing from Paul Ricoeur's notion of narrative identity, which links the formation of our identities to the narratives we construct about ourselves, Patel suggests that such interfaith narratives are critical ways through which communicators write themselves into the identity of an interfaith leader and activist (*Interfaith* 28-29). In narrating moments of enrichment, connection, conflict, cooperation, and difference with people or ideas from other (religious) traditions, writers and audiences are given opportunities to reflect on and reposition themselves in relation to other people, communities, and lines of thinking.

In the context of the writing classroom, rhetorical work of this kind could be highly valuable for extending the pedagogical approach I took in RRSW and for cultivating what Elizabeth Vander Lei calls an "attitude of renovation"—a disposition that "valu[es] what is present and seek[s] to improve it, over deciding to demolish it and build anew" (90). The value of such a disposition, Vander Lei suggests, is that "we might find ourselves and our students challenged to be willing to change our arguments as a result of encountering new people and ideas, to accept and even value heterogeneity and specificity in our discourse communities, and to evaluate proposed arguments in light of community standards" (92). Related to this, Vander Lei states, "If we help students, all students, recognize that their own stories are nested in larger stories, students may better apprehend the powerful rhetorical effect of those larger stories on their own. As a result, they may interrogate these larger stories and their effects more carefully" (97). Rhetorical work of this sort could no doubt go a long way toward promoting identification, connection, and relationship among writers of varied religious orientations.

As Patricia Roberts-Miller rightly asserts in *Deliberate Conflict: Argument, Political Theory, and Composition Classes*, "Deliberative democracy makes high demands of citizens." The demands are so high in fact that deliberative democratic engagement among diverse citizens seems nearly impossible at moments. As Roberts-Miller states, "The question is not whether it will go wrong, but whether or not it will go at all" (187). When religious diversity is acknowledged as a significant dimension of this universe of discourse, these demands are heightened. It is certainly possible that the increase of religious diversity in our contemporary moment has the potential to create new fractures and widen divisions among citizens. Our pluralistic religious landscape, however, also offers opportunities for engaging resources, wisdom, and approaches of traditions and communities that might enable citizens to cooperatively (and more effectively) address the complexities of our current moment. I am hopeful that teacher-scholars in our field will have a central role in preparing writers to seize the generative possibilities of the latter.

Works Cited

Allison, Jay and Dan Gediman, editors. *This I Believe II: the Personal Philosophies of Remarkable Men and Women*. Henry Holt and Company, 2008.

—. *This I Believe II: the Personal Philosophies of Remarkable Men and Women*. Henry Holt and Company, 2008.

Andrews, Elizabeth J. *Writing the Sacred Journey: The Art and Practice of Spiritual Memoir*. Skinner House Books, 2005.

Baca, Damian, et al., editors. *Landmark Essays on Rhetorics of Difference*. Routledge, 2019.

Bizzell, Patricia, and Bruce Herzberg, editors and authors. *Negotiating Difference: Cultural Case Studies for Composition*. Bedford, 1995.

Blankenship, Lisa. *Changing the Subject: A Theory of Rhetorical Empathy*. Utah State UP, 2019.

Booth, Wayne C. *The Rhetoric of RHETORIC: The Quest for Effective Communication*. Blackwell, 2004.

Brooks, David. *The Road to Character*. Random House, 2015.

Burke, Kenneth. *A Rhetoric of Motives*. U of California P, 1969.

Canagarajah, Suresh. *Translingual Practice: Global Englishes and Cosmopolitan Relations*. Routledge, 2013.

Clifton, Jennifer. *Argument as Dialogue Across Difference: Engaging Youth in Public Literacies*. Routledge, 2017.

Crowley, Sharon and Deborah Hawhee. *Ancient Rhetorics for Contemporary Students*. 5th ed., Pearson, 2011.

DePalma, Michael-John. "Re-envisioning Religious Discourses as Rhetorical Resources in Composition Teaching: A Pragmatic Response to the Challenge of Belief." *College Composition and Communication*, vol. 63, no. 2, 2011, pp. 219–43.

—. "Reimagining Rhetorical Education: Fostering Writers' Civic Capacities through Engagement with Religious Rhetorics." *College English*, vol. 79, no. 3, 2017, pp. 251–75.

Duffy, John. "Ethical Rhetoric in Unethical Times: Five Strategies for the Writing Class room." *Teacher-Scholar-Activist*, 30 April 2019, teacher-scholar-activist.org/2019/04/30/ethical-rhetoric-in-unethical-times-five-strategies-for-the-writing-classroom/.

—. "The Good Writer: Virtue Ethics and the Teaching of Writing." *College English*, vol. 79, no. 3, 2017, pp. 229–50.

Earle, Chris S. "Religion, Democracy, and Public Writing: Habermas on the Role of Religion in Public Life." *College English*, vol. 81, no. 2, 2018, pp. 133–54.

Foss, Sonja K., and Cindy L. Griffin. "Beyond Persuasion: A Proposal for an Invitational Rhetoric." *Communication Monographs*, vol. 62, no. 1, 1995, pp. 2–18.

Geiger, TJ, III. "Unpredictable Encounters: Religious Discourse, Sexuality, and the Free Exercise of Rhetoric." *College English*, vol. 75, no. 3, 2013, pp. 250–71.

Glenn, Cheryl, et al. *Rhetorical Education in America*. U Alabama P, 2009.

Hum, Sue, and Arabella Lyon. "Recent Advances in Comparative Rhetoric." *The Sage Handbook of Rhetorical Studies*, edited by Andrea Lunsford, et al. Sage, 2008, pp. 153–63.

Jones, Robert P., and Daniel Cox. "America's Changing Religious Identity: Findings from the 2016 American Values Atlas." Public Religion Research Institute, 2017. *PRRI.org*, www.prri.org/wp-content/uploads/2017/09/PRRI-Religion-Report.pdf.

Lewis, Earl, and Nancy Cantor. "Introduction." *Out of Many Faiths: Religious Diversity and the American Promise*. Princeton UP, 2018, pp. xi-xxi.

Mandelker, Amy and Elizabeth Powers, editors. *Pilgrim Souls: A Collection of Spiritual Autobiographies*. Touchstone, 1999.

Marty, Martin E. *The One and the Many: America's Struggle for the Common Good*. Harvard UP, 1997.

"Mission Statement." *Baylor University*, www.baylor.edu/about/index.php?id=88781. Accessed 23 March 2021.

Patel, Eboo. *Interfaith Leadership: A Primer*. Beacon Press, 2016.

—. "Toward a Field of Interfaith Studies." *Liberal Education*, vol. 99, no. 4, 2013, pp. 38–43.

Pew Forum on Religion and Public Life. "The Global Religious Landscape: A Report on the Size and Distribution of the World's Major Religious Groups as of 2010." Pew Research Center, 2012. *Pewforum.org*, www.pewforum.org/2012/12/18/global-religious-landscape-exec/.

—. "Religious Landscape Study." Pew Research Center, 2015. *Pewform.org*. www.pewforum.org/religious-landscape-study/.

Pratt, Mary Louis. "Arts of the Contact Zone." *Profession*, 1991, pp. 33–40.

Prelli, Lawrence J., editor. *Rhetorics of Display*. U of South Carolina P, 2006.

"Profile of Undergraduate Students: Fall 2018 and Fall 2019." *IRT Series*, vol. 19-20, no. 7, 13 Sept. 2019, www.baylor.edu/ir/doc.php/342532.pdf. Accessed 23 March 2021.

Ratcliffe, Krista. *Rhetorical Listening: Identification, Gender, Whiteness*. Southern Illinois UP, 2006.

Ringer, Jeffrey M. "The Dogma of Inquiry: Composition and the Primacy of Faith." *Rhetoric Review*, vol. 32, no. 3, 2013, pp. 349–65.

—. *Vernacular Christian Rhetoric and Civil Discourse: The Religious Creativity of Evangelical Student Writers*. Routledge, 2016.

Roberts-Miller, Patricia. *Deliberate Conflict: Argument, Political Theory, and Composition Classes*. Southern Illinois UP, 2004.

Tippett, Krista. *Speaking of Faith: Why Religion Matters—And How to Talk About It*. Penguin, 2007.

Trimbur, John. "Consensus and Difference in Collaborative Learning." *College English*, vol. 51, no. 6, 1989, pp. 602–16.

Vander Lei, Elizabeth. "Ain't We Got Fun?: Teaching Writing in a Violent World." *Renovating Rhetoric in Christian Tradition*, edited by Elizabeth Vander Lei, Thomas Amorose, Beth Daniell, and Anne Ruggles Gere, U of Pittsburgh P, 2014, pp. 89–104.

Williams, Mark Alan. "Transformations: Locating Agency and Difference in Student Accounts of Religious Experience." *College English*, vol. 77, no. 4, 2015, pp. 338–63.

Zaleski, Philip and Philip Yancey, editors. *The Best Spiritual Writing 2012*. Penguin Books, 2011.

JAEPL, Vol. 26, 2021

Acting with Inscriptions: Expanding Perspectives of Writing, Learning, and Becoming

Kevin Roozen

Abstract: *This article argues for increased attention to people's engagements with inscriptions and inscriptional practices and the long-term implications they have for the ongoing production of persons, practices, and social worlds across heterogeneous times, places, and activities. Based on a multi-year case study, this analysis examines one microbiology major's production and use of inscriptions at the intersections of his participation in both disciplinary science and religious worship and traces the long-term consequences those uses have for his becoming as a scientist of faith. If, as Paul Prior asserts, "literate activity is not located in acts of reading and writing but as cultural forms of life saturated with textuality, that is strongly motivated and mediated by texts," then we need to take seriously the full range of semiotic textualities and texts implicated in people's lives and their roles in people's meaning-making and becoming.*

In "Fuzzy Genres and Community Identities: The Case of Architecture Students' Sketchbooks," Peter Medway examines the functions that keeping and using sketchbooks play in the development of these students' ways of knowing and being. Borrowing from Bruno Latour and Steve Woolgar's notion of "inscriptions,"[1] a term they em-

---

1. In a footnote to chapter 2 of *Laboratory Life,* Latour and Woolgar state that their notion of "inscriptions" comes from Derrida, who used the term in reference to material representations "more basic than writing" (88). Latour and Woolgar use "inscriptions" to distinguish "all traces, spots, points, histograms, recorded numbers, spectra, peaks, and so on" that animate the work they observed in scientific laboratories (88) from the traditional kinds of published textual products, such as scientific articles and books, typically referred to as "writing." Other examples of inscriptions Latour and Woolgar offer throughout their book include "hastily drawn diagrams" (47), and "material dictionaries" such as "racks of samples, each of which bears a label with a 10-digit code number" and "files full of data sheets" (48), and "photographs" (88). In "The Role of Representations in Engineering Practices: Taking a Turn Toward Inscriptions," Aditya Johri, Wolff-Michael Roth, and Barbara Olds, use "inscription" as a term that "covers everything that is used to refer to some thing or phenomenon in the material world, including photographs, naturalistic drawings, diagrams, graphs, tables, lists, and equations" (8). In *Mind as Action,* James Wertsch offers a list of semiotic means that Vygotsky mentioned in his scholarship, including "various systems of counting; mnemonic techniques; algebraic symbol systems; works of art; writing; schemes, diagrams, maps and mechanical drawings," all of which Wertsch notes would be considered as material inscriptions in the sense that "they are physical objects that can be touched and manipulated. Furthermore, they can continue to exist as physical objects even when incorporated into the flow of action" (30). Writing

ploy in referring to the wide variety of material representations—from written alphabetic annotations to photographs, drawings, diagrams, charts, tables, lists, graphs, equations, instrument readings, and more—employed in scientists' meaning-making, Medway uses the term "inscriptional semiotic modes" (125) to describe the promiscuous blendings of handwritten alphabetic prose, drawings, diagrams, numbers, markings, and objects that texture the pages of architecture students' sketchbooks. Noting that such semiotic ensembles "do not fall neatly within a narrow definition of 'writing research' because they make use of other semiotic media as well, sometimes to the near exclusion of writing" (128), Medway says that people's engagements with such texts have gone largely unexamined in writing studies scholarship and suggests that researchers "need to move away from 'writing' as the focus of our studies and to acknowledge the importance of texts that are multimodal" (128).

Medway's chapter offers just one in a long history of calls for writing researchers to address the broad expanse of semiotic means that shape people's textual practices of meaning-making. Emerging from the 1966 Dartmouth conference, John Dixon's *Growth in English*, published in 1967, forwards an argument for resisting perspectives that offer "partial and incomplete view[s]" and "dangerous simplification[s]" (1) of the richness and variety of writing in people's lives. Challenging reductive views, Dixon argues for a more capacious perspective of 'writing' that could encompass a boy's diary entry about catching newts in a pond, a young girl's drawings and accompanying poem about a kitten, the diagrams and sketches involved in activities such as "a group of boys designing and making something like a go-kart" (67), the prose description generated by a young girl observing flower petals under a microscope, and the moving images and sounds of television programs and films. Twenty-five years later, in "Context, Text, Intertext: Toward a Constructivist Semiotic of Writing" Stephen Witte identifies the need for "a conceptualization of writing that is predicated on broader and … more realistic understandings of text and writing than have generally informed writing research to date" (238). Based on his review of writing research up to the two decades preceding 1992, Witte argues that

> Although traditional language, whether spoken or recorded in print, is clearly an important component in many meaning-making activities we have come to associate with the production and comprehension of traditional alphabetic text, attending only to traditional language will not permit us to account for either the production or use of many "written texts" we all encounter on a daily

---

Studies scholars might be more familiar with other kinds of texts addressed in writing studies scholarship that would be included under the broad category of inscriptions. In addition to the pages of the sketchbook pages examined by Peter Medway and the other examples I mention throughout this article, those texts would include the drawings on the calendar crafted by one of the students in Elizabeth Chiseri-Strater's *Academic Literacies,* the baseball cards used by Mary Louise Pratt's son and the manuscript by Guaman Poma discussed in "Arts of the Contact Zone," and the gang graffiti and posters on the boy's bedroom wall examined by Ralph Cintron in *Angels Town*. More recently, in "Who Has the Right to Write? Custodian Writing and White Property in the *University*," Calley Moratta addresses the tattoos of custodial employees.

basis—labels on cereal boxes, traffic signs, telephone book yellow pages, the operating manuals in the glove compartments of new automobiles …—all of which rely on non-linguistic sign systems. (240)

Ultimately, Witte asserts, a comprehensive framework for a viable understanding of writing would need to recognize that "to study writing is, over and above all else, to study acts of making meaning that are mediated through 'texts.' 'Texts' may be defined broadly as organized sets of symbols or signs" (237).

Twenty-five years after Witte's article, and fifty years after Dixon's book, Paul Prior notes in his 2017 *Research in the Teaching of English* forum response titled "Setting a Research Agenda for Lifespan Writing Development: The Long View from Where?" that despite the long history of calls for attention to the broader semiotic and multimodal dimensions of people's textual acting in the world, including Witte's, a focus on "just-writing," a term Prior uses to describe the emphasis on written alphabetic prose as the privileged semiotic mode, "continues to be the most common unit of analysis in research." As a corrective, Prior argues for an approach that takes "embodied, mediated, dialogic, semiotic practice as the basic unit of analysis" (215) in order to address people's efforts at meaning-making in ways that can include interweavings of semiotic performance across a wide array of modalities, including visual representations, bodily gesture and movement, musical expression, and mathematical calculation. Prior's argument for understanding and studying writing as embodied semiotic practice extends his earlier assertion in *Writing/Disciplinarity* for taking "literate activity," which he defines as "cultural forms of life saturated with textuality, that [are] strongly motivated and mediated by texts" (138) as a productive unit of analysis for examining people's concrete textual engagements in the world.

In the years since Prior's response, calls for increasingly capacious perspectives of writing have continued to texture writing studies scholarship. In *Queer Literacies: Discourses and Discontents*, published in 2019, Mark McBeth's examination of the broad range of literacy archives and artifacts Queer people have used to reshape their discursive and material selves and worlds reveals the wealth and variety of textualities—from crayon drawings to medical texts to making and marching with picket signs—that have been central to their efforts to "reinscribe themselves into the historical memory of culture and society" (233). In "Becoming Multilingual Writers through Translation," published in 2020, Xiqiao Wang's close, careful analysis of the translation practices of one transnational and multilingual undergraduate illuminates the lengthy and complex chains of multiple languages, digital tools, cultural narratives, rhetorical traditions, and learning trajectories that are continually woven, unwoven, and rewoven together across multiple semiotic repertoires.

This article echoes and extends writing studies' long history of calls for more capacious notions of the texts and textual practices that animate people's lives and actions. Based on data collected from a multi-year longitudinal case study of one writer throughout his college years (as well as recollections and artifacts from his early childhood), this analysis traces this student's engagement with inscriptions, specifically the diagrams that animate his science courses (see Figure 1 as an example), and the enduring consequences acting with inscriptions holds for his development as a scientist-in-the-making.

Fig. 1 An excerpt from a page of Samuel's organic chemistry notebook showing his efforts to graphically represent organic molecules. The representations depicted are chair conformation diagrams of cyclohexane molecules.

During the time of our research together, Samuel, a Black (his chosen term) undergraduate at a large public university in the southeast, was a microbiology major considering a career in veterinary medicine. As an undergraduate, his experience was initially textured by the tension he felt between his intense interest in science and his long history of engagement with religious worship. According to Samuel, his fascination with science began with the inquisitive nature he displayed as a child. As he described it, "growing up I always had a love for animals and I was always the thinker, always asked a bunch of questions." He noted, though, that "growing up in the area I grew up in, it wasn't cool to really pursue that, so like in my science classes, I really wasn't that interested in that." Through his volunteer work with a pet care center and his experiences in labs for his high school science classes, Samuel grew increasingly drawn to "just finding out how something works at the atomic level and molecular level and cellular and the tissue, organs, developing into the organism and how all of that works." By the middle of high school, Samuel indicated that he "just fell in love with biology. I was able to immerse myself in it. And I'm like, 'I'm really good at this'." His experiences with animals eventually drew him toward college and veterinary medicine.

The one thing that gave Samuel serious pause about a career in science was its potential impact on his deep engagement with the church, a vital part of his upbringing and family life. Members of Samuel's family were active in the Black Presbyterian church they have attended for generations. Both of his parents held positions in the church leadership, and Samuel and his brother had been involved with church activities since their early childhood. Recalling the tension he felt about maintaining his faith and presence in the church as his budding interest in science grew, Samuel stated,

> When I first started really pursuing science, I had trouble trying to see science and God in the same vein because of the way our culture works. We see them as two polarized, very opposite entities, that you can't pursue knowledge of the world or try to understand creation and God himself.... All of the people that I would talk to would be like either, "Yes! Science is the answer, science is the way, science gives me all of the answers that I could ever possibly need to know." And then others were like, "No, science is not this. You can't believe that all of this makes sense."

Faced with the dichotomy offered by this powerful cultural narrative, Samuel considered forsaking his interest in science for what he described as a "steady job" that would allow him to stay actively involved in his church. At the point Samuel started college, he shifted his stance, reconciling himself to keeping his religious engagement fairly private while pursuing his goal to become a vet. In this article, I argue that acting with inscriptions offers Samuel ways of knowing and being in the world that productively entangle his science and religious experiences, and that these interweavings have had long-term implications for his becoming as a scientist of faith.

Looking with Literate Activity

To gain some purchase on Samuel's engagement with the inscriptions he encountered in his science coursework, I take up Prior's invitation to attend to "literate activity." Drawing upon theoretical perspectives that posit human activity as mediated by people acting with semiotic tools in situated moments and along historical chains of action (Bakhtin; Wertsch, *Voices*; Voloshinov; Vygotsky), in *Writing/Disciplinarity* Prior proposes literate activity as a unit of analysis that could better account for the many cultural tools, practices, actors (humans and non-humans), and activities dispersed throughout the lengthy histories that come to be entangled in people's textual engagements typically referred to as "writing" and "reading." Defining literate activity "not as located in acts of reading and writing, but as cultural forms of life saturated with textuality, that is strongly motivated and mediated by texts" (138), Prior's use of the terms "textualities" and "texts" explicitly signals the incredible diversity of material and cultural practices that mediate communicative action, including those offered among the many examples of "written inscriptions" listed by Prior and Charles Bazerman in their introductory chapter to *What Writing Does and How It Does It*. These examples range from "a name carved into a stone monument or into a tree" to "an animated banner running across a Web page" to "an income tax form" (Bazerman and Prior 7). Those terms also speak to how "communicative practices are multimodal—with talk, text, bodily stance and gesture, graphics, mathematics, and other symbolic activity woven together through interactional history" (Prior, *Writing/Disciplinarity* 70). The attention to the broad multimodality of texts people act with is reiterated in Prior and Jody Shipka's "Chronotopic Lamination: Tracing the Contours of Literate Activity," where they write that literate activity "is about representational practices, complex, multifarious chains of transformations in and across representational states and media" (181-182). Literate activity, then, provides a way to move beyond reductive conceptions of the kinds of texts typically associated with "writing" and "reading" in order to more fully address the broad array of inscriptions, regardless of semiotic modality, implicated in people's representational practices, the incredible variety of inscriptions that people act with.[2] As a construct for understanding and studying writing, literate activity works to resist arbitrarily reducing people's efforts at meaning-making solely in terms of their engagement with a narrow range of texts that privilege a particular semiotic mode.

Situated studies of writing have productively taken up a literate activity perspective to examine people's semiotic performances with the variety of material texts, including notations, diagrams, puzzles, and games that are linked into the invention and production of academic publications (Durst; Prior, *Writing/Disciplinarity*; Prior and Shipka; Roozen, "Coming to Act"; Shipka); patient documents, medical and everyday illustrations, and visual images used to understand and monitor physical health (Bellwoar); blendings of visual images and prose employed in social media postings (Buck; Wang); drawings, both print and digital, for participating in fan activities (Fraiberg, "Pretty Bullets"; Roozen, "'Fan fic-ing'"); the blendings of visual images and multiple languages, both spoken and written, animating workplace meetings (Fraiberg, "Composition 2.0"); and the interweaving of diagrams, images, objects, and gestures used in designing a computer interface for an interactive website (Prior, "ReMaking IO"; "Writing").

Because of its focus on people's concrete experiences with specific semiotic tools, the lens of literate activity helps us understand how people, acts, and objects come to be entangled in and across heterogeneous activities. To conceptualize the way literate acts come to be textured by an accumulated and ever-accumulating heterogeneity and heterochronicity of social action, Prior draws upon Erving Goffman's notion of lamination—the way multiple, heterogeneous social frames and footings are dynamically and agentively woven into moments of action; how multiple activities co-exist, are immanent, in any situation. Rather than separate layers of thin veneer, lamination conceptualizes such interweavings as densely entangled and interanimating. In this sense, a literate activity perspective makes visible how people's engagement with a particular text, according to Prior, is "not only multimodal, but also temporally and spatially dispersed and distributed across multiple persons, artifacts, and sites" (*Writing/Disciplinarity* 137). Each moment of textual action, Prior notes, "implicates multiple activities, weaves together histories, and exists within the … networks of lifeworlds where boundaries of time and

---

2. For Prior, the term "act with" ("Sociocultural" 55) highlights an explicit recognition that action is accomplished by people acting with cultural tools. In examining people's literate activities, "act with" also serves as a way of explicitly signaling the many ways people interact with texts that can be easily obscured by terms such as "writing" and "reading."

space are highly permeable" (277). Prior and Shipka define the laminated character of literate activity as "the dispersed, fluid chains of places, times, people, and artifacts that come to be tied together in trajectories of literate action along with the ways multiple activity footings are held and managed" (181), and offer a number of analyses that illuminate how people's uses of texts and artifacts are simultaneously linked into multiple, seemingly disparate activities, including, for example, how domestic activities such as doing family laundry and leisure pursuits such as playing board games and puzzles are connected to the invention and production of disciplinary writing. This tangling of textual engagements across heterogeneous activities, Prior and Shipka contend, is a central way that literate activity functions for people to "not only inhabit made-worlds, but constantly make our worlds—the ways we select from, (re)structure, fiddle with, and transform the material and social worlds we inhabit" (182).

According to Prior and Shipka, this laminated quality arises from the fact that multiple activities are "co-genetic," or "co-developing," that elements from one domain are "always developing in association with other activities, actions, and artifacts" (207) no matter how different or disconnected those activities might seem. A literate activity perspective, then, invites consideration of the ways any focal activity develops in conjunction with, rather than apart from, other activities. This co-development of activities, and of people and the semiotic tools they act with, creates what Prior refers to as "affordances for alignment" (*Writing/Disciplinarity* 277), conditions which can occasion further agentive entanglings of social worlds and people's histories with them. In this sense, literate activity alerts us to how people's textualities emerge from heterogeneously textured lifeworlds and how those lifeworlds are continually woven together, unwoven, and rewoven again throughout people's lifespans.

With regard to how people come to act with texts in the world, then, a focus on literate activity highlights the wide array of semiotic tools people act with (e.g., spoken and written languages, images, gesture, embodied performance), both as they are combined and coordinated within emerging moments of situated action and chained together across time and space. It also illuminates how people and the semiotic artifacts they act with are continually being heterogeneously entangled with new elements for new purposes. In "How Do Moments Add up to Lives?" Prior argues that these features of literate activity are central for understanding what he refers to as people's "trajectories of semiotic becoming," the continually emergent, richly embodied, complexly mediated, and heterogeneously dispersed pathways of development people trace throughout their lifespans and across their lifeworlds. In contrast to narrow, static models of development that cast learning and socialization in terms of people's use of any single semiotic modality and in any single homogeneous social world, Prior writes that "Becoming happens in spaces that are never pure or settled, where discourses and knowledge are necessarily heterogeneous, and where multiple semiotic resources are so deeply entangled that distinct modes simply don't make sense" (Introduction). For Prior, the heterogeneously textured artifacts, practices, and identities that are assembled in laminated moments of "intra-action" (Barad 33) function as the resources for meaning, agency, and action that people build from in later moments in the near and distant futures.

Methods

When my study with Samuel began, he had just started his second year of college. I first came to know him as a student in a class I was teaching. During that semester, Samuel indicated that he was a microbiology major immersed in a wealth of literate activity for his science coursework. The following semester, I invited him to participate in a research study to understand the textual practices he was using. As the research moved forward, Samuel took up the role of "co-researcher" (Ivanic 110) in the sense that, understanding the goals of the study, he brought new data in to interviews, suggested topics of discussion, offered his own insights, and responded constructively and critically to my emerging understandings. Initially, I collected sample texts from and conducted text-based interviews regarding his classes. During our early interviews, Samuel often mentioned his religious faith (e.g., his knowledge of the Bible, his parents' roles in the church they attended) and his activities associated with religious worship (e.g., attending church services, studying and memorizing religious texts, singing religious songs). Because I sensed that his faith and these related activities were important to him, and because such faith-based activities also figured prominently in my own history, both as part of my family life and throughout extended periods of my K-12 schooling, these subjects became something we talked about during our interviews.

Subsequent interviews led to more focused examinations of Samuel's practices, and included collection of sample texts in whatever representational media were appropriate (e.g., hard copy and digital inscriptions). Collecting sample texts was crucial for process- and practice-based interviews focused on making visible how and why Samuel created and used specific texts. Process-based interviews involved having Samuel create retrospective accounts (often supported by texts and other artifacts) of the processes involved in the invention, production, and circulation of a particular text (e.g., the current draft of one of Samuel's chemistry lab reports), and key elements (e.g., other people or texts, inscriptional tools and technologies) involved in those processes. Practice-based interviews aimed at understanding why and how such elements were employed.

In all, we conducted eight formal interviews, which resulted in just over 14 hours of video and audiotape data. I supplemented the formal interviews with dozens of follow-up questions developed while I examined the interview recordings, my notes, and texts that Samuel provided. I emailed these follow-up questions to Samuel after the formal interviews, and he either emailed his responses, brought them up during later formal interviews, or mentioned them during informal conversations when he stopped by my office or during chance meetings on campus. This ongoing series of interviews provided opportunities for the kinds of "longer conversations" and "cyclical dialogue around texts over a period of time" that Theresa Lillis (362) identified as crucial for understanding literate practice within the context of a participant's history. They also allowed for what Amy Stornaiuolo, Anna Smith, and Nathan Phillips describe as "the unprecedented, surprising, and meaningful to emerge in observations of human activity without predetermined and text-centric endpoints of explanations" (78). One insight that slowly emerged from our series of conversations and exchanges was Samuel's frequent use of diagrams and other inscriptions and their prominent importance in his science coursework as well as his other textual engagements. In terms of his science coursework, for example, I noticed how fully he was immersed in an extensive cascade of inscriptions for his biology and chemistry classes and labs. I also noticed how frequently talk about diagrams and other inscriptions related to his various science courses emerged during our interviews, and how frequently during our discussions he would draw out the diagrams he mentioned and how quickly he generated them as a form of what Laurence Musgrove and Myra Musgrove describe, via their own graphic illustration, as "handmade thinking" people use to "to understand and to be understood" (92). Because of my own experiences taking science courses in primary and secondary school, and then briefly pursuing a biology major and working for a short time as a lab assistant in a microbiology lab during college, these inscriptions became topics of discussion during our interviews.

In order to focus on Samuel's engagement with diagrams, I oriented my analysis toward the histories of his use of inscriptions and inscriptional practices. I analyzed these data interpretively and holistically (Durst; Miller, Hengst, and Wang; Prior, *Writing/Disciplinarity*). I first arranged data representations (i.e., sample texts, sections of interview transcripts, interpretive notes, copies of images, printed versions of still images captured from video, drawings Samuel had created during interviews, etc.) chronologically in the order in which Samuel engaged with them throughout his lifespan. Those data representations were examined for instances where I sensed, or Samuel indicated that, he was acting with particular inscriptions or employing particular inscriptional practices.

This analysis of the data generated a number of histories, what Catherine Kell refers to as "meaning-making trajectories" ("Making"; "Literacy"; see also Bellwoar) that stretched across seemingly different literate activities throughout Samuel's life. Based on those histories, I constructed brief initial narratives of his use of particular inscriptions across multiple engagements. Those initial narratives were reviewed and modified by checking and re-checking those constructions against the data representations (to ensure accuracy and seek counter instances) and by submitting them to Samuel for his examination. At these times I often requested additional texts from Samuel, and frequently he volunteered to provide additional materials and insights that he thought might be useful in further elaborating and extending the narratives. Frequently my understanding of Samuel's use of inscriptions for different literate activities needed significant modification as a result of closer inspection of the data, identification of additional relevant data, or discussions with Samuel during interviews or via email. Accounts of these interactions were modified according to Samuel's feedback. Finally, Samuel was invited to member check final versions of the narratives in order to determine if they seemed valid from his perspective.

Samuel's Acting with Inscriptions

As a sophomore microbiology major with a career goal of veterinary medicine, Samuel found himself deeply immersed in a dense landscape of inscriptions. Samuel's lectures, textbooks, and notes for his initial chemistry courses, for example, were saturated with diagrams, especially the various diagrams of molecules that his professors drew on the whiteboard and that he himself drew in his lecture notebook and for his homework assignments and exams. Articulating the centrality of inscriptions as the locus of the scientific enterprise, Latour writes, "Scientists start seeing something once they stop looking at nature and look exclusively and obsessively at prints and flat inscriptions" (39). What might seem like errant doodles or a simplistic shorthand are, as Latour states, "innovations in graphism" (29) that are key semiotic tools in "the precise practice and craftsmanship of knowing" (21) for chemistry. Discussing the importance of these diagrams for the development of disciplinary practice for chemistry, Latour writes,

> The manipulation of substances in gallipots and alambics becomes chemistry only when all the substances can be written in a homogeneous language where everything is simultaneously presented to the eye. The writing of words inside a classification are not enough. Chemistry becomes powerful only when a visual vocabulary is invented that replaces the manipulations by calculation and formulas. Chemical structure can be drawn, composed, broken apart on paper, like music or arithmetic, all the way to Mendeleiev's table. (36)

According to Latour, acting with these inscriptions, coming to interpret them, name them, generate them, see them, is essentially the work of a chemist, and learning how to create and see with these inscriptions is a key part of Samuel's rhetorical education as a scientist-in-the-making.

Drawing diagrams played an especially important role in Samuel's organic chemistry class. From the very beginning of the course, much of the activity centered around acting with a variety of molecular diagrams, bare-bones depictions that "present to the eye" a molecule's key relevant features and its spatial arrangement and allow molecules to be "drawn, composed" and "broken apart on paper," like the ones shown on the page from Samuel's organic chemistry notebook offered in Figure 2.

Describing the kinds of "interpretive journeys"[3] involving these inscriptions that his professor would offer during class lectures, for example, Samuel indicated that she

> doesn't write too, too much on the board unless it's drawing a structure.... Like a Newman projection, she'll draw that on the board. Like an organic structure she may draw on the board and then talk about chirality of a compound. 2-bromobutane [pointing to the diagram at the top right of the page from his

---

3. In their article "Interpretive Journeys: How Physicists Talk and Travel through Graphic Space," Elinor Ochs, sally Jacoby, and Patrick Gonzalez use the term "interpretive journey" to describe scientists' common practice of drawing an inscription on a surface such as a chalkboard, and then animating that inscription with their talk and gestures. It is through this practice, the authors note, that "scientists take seemingly immutable inscriptions … and over narrative time, transform them into highly mutable, highly intertextual and symbolic narrative spaces through which they verbally, gesturally, and graphically journey" (158). I employ this term as a way of helping readers to keep in mind that in the lectures he attends, Samuel is not just encountering, and acting with, an inert inscription that his professors draw on a whiteboard. Rather, Samuel is encountering an inscription as it is linked into his professor's talk, gestures, gaze, bodily stance, and likely to other inscriptions that have also been drawn on the board, as well as those that have been recently erased during the class meeting, and those offered in the textbook and other course materials.

notebook pictured in Figure 1, above] is one of her favorites. At least for showing stereoisomers.

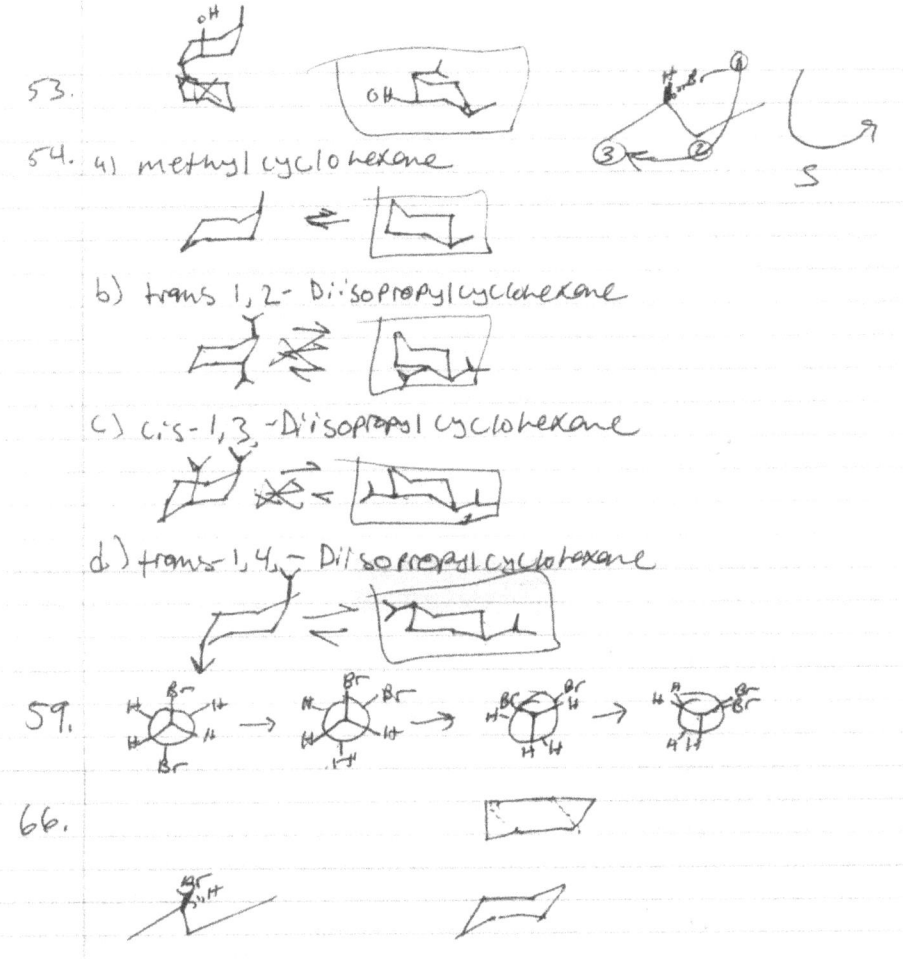

Fig. 2 A page from Samuel's notes for his organic chemistry class. The series of diagrams listed for items 53 and 54 are a series of chair conformation diagrams. The series of diagrams next to item 59 are Newman projection diagrams. The skeletal structure diagram for 2-bromobutane, one of Samuel's professor's "favorite" structures to draw, appears at the top right and bottom left-hand side of the page.

Samuel indicated that he was somewhat surprised at the emphasis placed on students being able to draw the diagrams themselves. I include below a brief excerpt from one of our interviews during which Samuel describes his organic chemistry professor's emphasis on knowing how to draw chair conformation diagrams:

Samuel: I don't write very neatly and I don't draw very well. So the fact that I had to draw these chair conformations [the diagrams in Figure 2 with the boxes drawn around them] in pen is just weird. Plus, like, one example of drawing them, like learning how do it … She taught us to set up each of these. [Samuel picks up a pen and draws the top of the two chair conformation diagrams at the very bottom right-hand side of the page shown in Figure 2] draw 2 parallel lines, set them each apart, and then draw an equilateral triangle. Well, whenever I would do it like that, my chair confirmations would come out looking like this [laughing, and pointing to the top conformation diagram he drew at the bottom of the page]. And I'm like, I don't understand!

KR: I see. So you're trying to get it to look like this [pointing to one of the chair conformation diagrams in the middle of the page].

Samuel: So I learned, ok if I do this and draw this up and draw this down, just do dramatic everything then it comes out looking like a chair conformation [drawing the chair conformation diagram at the very bottom right-hand side of the page].

KR: And she actually had to teach people in class, like, this is how to do the chair conformation?

Samuel: The book does it one way, she does it another way and I was just like.

KR: How does the book do it?

Samuel: It's weird. It says something about drawing a deep V. Here it is [pointing to a page of his textbook]. Draw this V then a line cutting the V in half, then draw a dramatic line going into the, in the plane, then back up, then, just weird, five different steps. Drawing it all in pieces.

In this portion from the interview, Samuel describes and illustrates no fewer than three different techniques he has encountered for drawing chair conformation diagrams. The first strategy, shown to him by his professor, involves drawing two slightly offset parallel lines and connecting them with two equilateral triangles. His comments regarding the second strategy suggest that it is a version of the first technique but involves drawing sharper, more "dramatic" triangles. The third approach, described and illustrated in his course textbook, involves a five-step process of drawing a series of deep "v" shapes and bisecting them.

As Latour notes, inscriptions are so "mundane," "so practical, so modest, so pervasive, so close to the hands and the eyes that they escape attention" (21). And yet it is through these mixtures of semiotic tools that chemists can represent molecules that cannot be seen with the naked eye and that are messy and confusing to make out even when they are made visible by cutting edge imaging technologies. With a "visual vocabulary" consisting of a few short line segments, simple geometric shapes (a circle, a solid, a set of short dashes), letters in the form of abbreviations for elements and combined with words and numbers for naming the molecules, these diagrams "present to the eye" a neat and precisely arranged structure. The simple shapes employed in the diagrams Samuel acts with offer up an image of precise order. In fact, given the simplicity of the shapes and symbols being deployed, it would be difficult for these diagrams *not* to present order and precision. The precise ordering is what allows chemists to see features like the positioning of particular atoms and the angles of the various bonds between them. These features, in turn, afford chemists a way of understanding how bonds are likely to change in response to interactions with other molecules, or how easily bonds might be formed or broken.

While these kinds of diagrams certainly allowed Samuel to see the key features and arrangements of molecules, they also presented to his eye a great deal more. According to Prior, the laminated nature of literate activity means that people's engagements with texts lead to "hybrid actions and understandings" that emerge from the "weav[ing] together [of] personal, interpersonal, artifactual, institutional, and sociocultural as well as disciplinary histories" (*Writing/Disciplinarity* xii). For Samuel, whose history includes a deep and sustained engagement with religious worship, his ability to see, use, and construe scientific diagrams was interwoven with, and thus shaped by, his engagement with his faith. Over multiple interviews, Samuel routinely mentioned how these renderings illuminated God's handiwork to him. His laminated seeing of chemical inscriptions surfaced quite unexpectedly, for example, during one of our interviews while discussing what he referred to as his "scripture box," a small box containing a series of three by five-inch index cards on which he had copied some Bible passages he was memorizing and written some of his own comments. I include below an excerpt from that interview, during which we discussed a passage from Colossians:

Samuel: So Colossians 1:17, [reading from an index card with the verse written on it]

> "He is before all things and in him all things hold together." …There's nothing apart from him, literally nothing apart from him because everything, institutions, atoms, subatomic particles, everything holds together in Christ.

KR: I can see why you chose that one.

Samuel: And then when people ask me why I believe what I believe or why I think the way I think I say, Hey, well, here's what the Bible tells me and it actually makes a lot of sense when you study like chemistry, we learn how the trend for the universe is randomness but the very nature of matter, even at the most seemingly insignificant of levels, the microscopic levels, there's organization. There's organization that we can actually notice plus there's still things that we don't understand about the organization and the structure of an atom, of the nucleus, of orbitals or electrons. We can't tell with any true 100% certainty where an electron is around an atom in orbit. And that becomes increasingly difficult when we talk about hybridization and the bonding that occurs between an SP3 orbital and an SP3 orbital like in ethane. Carbon carbon sigma bond is in SP3 orbital. We know that the electrons are somewhere in here but the bond angle is greater than the atomic radius of one carbon. So we don't' know for certain, with even less certainty where it is.

After reading the verse, Samuel elaborates the phrase "all things hold together" by emphasizing that "all things" encompasses "institutions, atoms, and subatomic particles." Following my brief comment about his decision to choose Colossians 1:17, Samuel then indicates that everything being held together by a divine maker is consistent with what the study of chemistry has illuminated regarding the ordered design of even the smallest levels of organization for the physical world. As examples, he evokes the structure of the atom and its constituents and the bonds between the carbon atoms in a molecule of ethane, structures typically represented in the diagrams he would have encountered during lectures for his science courses, on the pages of his course textbooks, and in the materials provided in the course's online resources, and inscribed on the pages of his notebook. For Samuel the organization and order "at the microscopic levels" made visible by diagrams depicting the sp3 bonding in ethane, for example, evidence God's ability to "hold all things together."

Samuel's heterogeneously distributed seeing of chemical inscriptions also surfaced unexpectedly during a later interview as we discussed his studying strategies. Explaining how he made sense of the complicated content of his organic chemistry courses, he stated,

> With organic, I see nuclearphilic attacks, electrophilic attacks, things of that nature, carbohydride shifts, hydride shifts. Like, I can visualize that in my head and so I see that in terms of anime and video games. And then when I get to see major product versus minor product, what's more stable, what's less stable, I'm like, oh, that makes sense because, hey, our God is a God of order, our God is a God of structure and so it makes sense that this membered ring would be favored over, say, a seven-membered ring which is all wobbly and unstable. Six-membered ring, you can have different chair confirmations, you can do just a whole bunch of really cool things with it so it makes more sense for the structure to favor it versus that. And also five-membered rings. They're fine, too. Which is why our DNA is comprised of a five-membered carbon sugar because ribose is six-membered…. You get to see all of the order in it so, like, with me it just makes everything make more sense.

After commenting that he understands various kinds of molecular "attacks" and "shifts" in terms of how characters interact in the anime he reads and video games he plays, Samuel explains that he makes sense of nature's tendency toward the more stable five and six-membered cyclohexane rings, which he had invested no small amount of time drawing and examining, in light of his understanding of God's tendency toward structure and order. The stability made visible in the comparing structural diagrams of six-membered rings to those of seven-membered rings evidenced for him the structure and order inherent in God's design.

To echo Latour, science is not all that Samuel is seeing or doing when he looks exclusively and obsessively at the inscriptions animating his science coursework. Samuel's engagements with these and other diagrams entangle his experience of disciplinary science with his long history of religious worship. While these linkages might seem like fleeting happenstance co-minglings of two distinctly different homogeneous social activities and worlds, we might instead view them as Samuel's laminated encounters with inscriptions in light of the complex heterogeneity of his history with both religion and disciplinary science. On the one hand, Samuel's laminated seeing of these inscriptions is supported by his engagement with the Black church that has figured so prominently in his life. In her chapter in *Literacy in American Lives* titled "'The Power of It': Sponsors of Literacy in African American Lives," (see also "Accumulating Literacy"), Deborah Brandt indicates that the church has functioned as "the most essential cultural institution for the well-being of African Americans since their forced arrival on this continent" (110-111). As a literacy sponsor, the Black church promotes "certain meanings, styles, postures, and inflections that reflect a unique racial history ... a set of interpretations and values that ... can shape reading and writing in many direct, indirect, and long-lasting ways" (145). As Brandt discovered during her research, one particularly salient feature of the Black church's sponsorship of its members' literacy practices is the idea that "religious and secular values and styles can coexist with the same practice or the same interpretive stance" (143), an orientation toward literate practice which affords "a multiplicity and simultaneity to the meanings of literacy—a synergy that often combines practical and spiritual significance and that makes one meaning less compelling without the other" (123). According to Brandt, this connection "works against the rather sharp divisions between secular and religious literacy that widened generally through the twentieth century" (118).

Brandt offers Jordan Grant (whom she refers to as Charles Randolph in "Accumulating Literacy"), the son of an African American preacher, as an example of how this orientation shapes a literate life. Tracing Grant's encounters with writing throughout his lifespan, Brandt notes how his father's style of writing sermons informed the prose in Grant's high school essays, the papers he crafted as an undergraduate English major, the reports he wrote for his administrative job, the pages of his doctoral dissertation, and the presentations he created for his current job as a consultant. It seems reasonable to surmise that the same relationship between spiritual and secular inspired by the church that animates Grant's encounters with literacy is also at play in Samuel's, even though their respective inscriptions emphasize different semiotic modes. Samuel did not mention that the Black churches he attended throughout his life offered sermons or lectures about the interweaving of faith and science. He did indicate, though, that the church he attended during his time at college had a mentoring program for new members, and the mentor he was assigned and met frequently with was a Black "scientist of faith." These heterogeneities texturing his engagements with religious worship would seem to afford Samuel's laminated seeing of scientific diagrams.

In addition, Samuel's identifications of God's handiwork in these kinds of inscriptions are also supported by his encounters with a number of science teachers and professors throughout his experiences in high school and college. Some of those encounters quite explicitly linked science and religion. While talking about some of the "people of faith" he had met in his science classes, for example, Samuel mentioned that he and one of his high school chemistry teachers, "would talk about God and we would talk about science all of the time. Just all of the time." Describing one particular instance in that class, Samuel mentioned that the teacher was showing "a picture of a neuron" to examine the neuron's myelin sheath and the fact that the charge impulse is stimulated by the uptake and release of sodium and calcium into the cell, and it releases neurotransmitters. It does this at a constant rate, a rate which we could never quite process. And all of those things turn into thoughts and or functions.

Commenting on the precisely ordered elegance depicted in the picture, his teacher asked the class, "How could people look at this and not say that that's the tapestry of God?" Other encounters Samuel mentioned were less explicit, such as when one of his undergraduate chemistry professors mentioned during a lecture that the Higgs Boson particle was commonly referred to as "the God particle," or when his undergraduate physics professor gifted Samuel a French translation of the Bible when Samuel mentioned to him that he had enrolled in a summer study-abroad program in Paris. Many of the other encounters Samuel brought up simply highlighted his teachers' openness to discuss religious issues. While talking about his undergraduate biology lab, for example, Samuel stated that he and the post doc leading the lab section "talk about pretty much everything. Any question I would have I would go to him about it. At one point we had a discussion on attributes of God and intelligent design and how evolution may or may not play a part in it." These interanimations of science and faith would also seem to support Samuel's laminated seeing of the diagrams he encountered in his coursework.

From a literate activity perspective, in weaving together his interest in science and his history of religious worship as he acts with inscriptions, Samuel is taking advantage of the co-genetic linkages, the affordances for alignment, that are already woven into his experiences with the church and in his science coursework. Rather than emerging solely from his encounters with disciplinary science, Samuel's seeing of the ethane, cyclohexane, and nerve cells is heterogeneously situated across and complexly mediated by his engagements with both science and the orientation to African American spirituality sponsored by the Black church. One important consequence of this lamination for Samuel is that it creates opportunities for him to draw his faith together with his science and his science together with his faith. Acting with inscriptions, in other words, occasions for Samuel what Gesa Kirch describes as "rich dimensions of reflection, introspection, and contemplation which lead us to know and understand things beyond the analytical mind" needed to "nourish and sustain an inner life" (58).

Toward Potential Futures

Just as Samuel's encounters with inscriptions in his near and distant past functioned as resources for present moments of action during his initial undergraduate science courses, the heterogeneity that textured those encounters also propelled action toward Samuel's potential futures. I turn now to elaborating how Samuel's laminated seeings of scientific inscriptions continued to inform his literate activity and his semiotic becoming throughout his final year at college and his graduate veterinary program.

One prominent way that Samuel's acting with inscriptions shaped his literate activity as an undergraduate is visible in the thesis he researched and wrote throughout his senior year, a project for which he examined the relationship between science and religion. Framed as a kind of overview of his development as a scientist of faith over his four years of college, Samuel's thesis offers readers some glimpses into his own experiences navigating this relationship. In contrast to the dominant cultural narrative that he described in his theses as viewing science and faith as "mutually exclusive or at the very least thought to operate in vastly different spheres such that one ought not to influence the other," Samuel wrote that by his senior year of college he had come to view them as existing in a productive resonance. Articulating his central argument in his abstract, Samuel writes, "the relationship between science and faith seems to be a synergistic one: the two enhance one another. As individuals study both the book of nature and the book of scripture, their love of God and enthusiasm for science are both enhanced."

In the opening portion of his thesis, Samuel indicates that he arrived at his conclusion by observing that science and faith had enriched one another in a number of ways in his life as an undergraduate: "As I began to grow in my knowledge of God and the Scriptures, I was also growing in my knowledge of biology and chemistry.... As I studied science more deeply, He seemed more fascinating, more brilliant, and more beautiful than I'd first realized. This, in turn, made me want to study science even more so that I could see more of the awesomeness of God." Over the next thirty-nine pages, Samuel points to a number of particular instances in which science and faith had come to be entangled in his life, reaching back to his initial years as an undergraduate. Each of the instances Samuel describes involved his close encounters with inscriptions.

In one passage, reflecting on the introductory science courses he took during his initial year as a microbiology major, Samuel writes,

> By viewing science in light of the sovereignty of God, I grew increasingly fond of Him and His creative genius. In each of my biology and chemistry courses, the incredible complexity and intricacy of the various systems that allow living beings, animals and microbes alike, to function left me in an incredible state of awe. Far too often I would find it rather difficult to contain my elation as my professors outlined these systems in great detail. Many times these observations simply made sense in light of the Character of God as expressed through the Scriptures.

In this passage, Samuel indicates that it was the "incredible complexity and intricacy of the various systems that allow living beings, animals and microbes alike, to function" presented to his eye through the many inscriptions in his biology and chemistry classes that provided him with a view of "the character of God." For Samuel, viewing "science in light of the sovereignty of God" not only helped him make sense of the complex systems represented in the diagrams, but also enhanced his appreciation for "His creative genius."

In a passage from his concluding chapter, in which he reflects on the full arc of his trajectory across the undergraduate curriculum, Samuel writes,

> As I have studied science, from biology to biochemistry, I have become more fascinated by the God I had come to know through the scriptures. Studying His character and seeing some of His characteristics reflected through the ways in which the elegant molecular systems that allow all of life to function at times overwhelms me with elation. Many times I can barely contain my joy and awestruck wonder as more and more of the power, genius, and creativity of

> God become apparent through the study of the book of nature. It drives me to love and follow Him more fervently with my heart, mind, and soul, while simultaneously making me more eager to study the science through which these attributes emanate.

Here, Samuel indicates that it was through examining "the elegant molecular systems that allow life to function" made readily visible through the inscriptions he encountered in courses "from biology to biochemistry" that he became "fascinated by the God I had come to know through the scriptures." For Samuel, the "elegant systems" made visible by the inscriptions reflected "the power, genius, and creativity of God." This increased insight into the character of the Creator also motivated Samuel to engage more deeply with "the science through which these attributes emanate."

Latour suggests that the ordinary, practical, and ubiquitous nature of inscriptions can make them easy to overlook, but that was certainly not the case with Samuel. Those seemingly mundane encounters with inscriptions held some enduring consequences for Samuel's becoming as a scientist-in-the-making. For Samuel, multiple entanglements with these inscriptions across multiple courses brought science and religion together for him. Based on what he describes throughout his thesis, the interweaving of science and religion was not just something he did initially in his early science courses and that eventually subsided as he progressed through the curriculum, something that faded as his participation with science deepened. Rather, it increasingly intensified. Over four years, Samuel's laminated seeing of diagrams deepened and enriched not just his knowledge of science, but also his "affective intensities" (Leander and Boldt) that motivated him to know more about science. In turn, his enriched view of science also deepened his affective intensities supporting his desire for knowing more about God's character.

Those laminated encounters with inscriptions also occasioned a crucial discursive space across which he could inscribe faith into his science and his science into his faith. In the pages of his thesis, Samuel's engagement with inscriptions, now indexed by and entextualized in his prose descriptions, enabled him to write himself into the long tradition of people like Galileo and Jonathan Edwards who developed a synergistic relationship between faith and science. Over four years, Samuel, who initially "had trouble trying to see science and God in the same vein" and who opted to background his faith to pursue a career in science, shifted his orientation to become a scientist of faith. The importance of both science and faith in shaping Samuel's becoming cannot be overstated. The biographical statement he crafted for the front matter of his thesis is especially telling in this regard. Offering a third-person overview of his accomplishments throughout his undergraduate years, he writes,

> He was involved in ministry on campus leading Bible studies for his residence hall, ministry and evangelism small groups, and various prayer meetings. His major area of study was Microbiology, and he studied French Language as his minor. After graduation, he will study veterinary medicine at [name of university] in the fall of 2014.

It is significant that Samuel leads by announcing his religious engagements *before* indicating his academic major and minor and *before* noting that he would attending veterinary school.

This trajectory of interanimating science and faith continued as Samuel navigated four years of veterinary school. During that time, Samuel led a large weekly Bible study for members of his cohort, and also co-facilitated a smaller Bible study as his schedule allowed. In addition, he was also deeply involved with some of the Christian veterinary organizations on his campus. Samuel graduated from veterinary school in Spring 2018, and soon afterwards started work as a veterinarian in a large city near his hometown. He also joined and became an active member of one of the nearby churches, and, as his busy schedule permits, he has continued his participation with the religiously affiliated veterinary medicine organizations at his alma mater.

In *Identity and Agency in Cultural Worlds,* Dorothy Holland, William Lachicotte, Debra Skinner, and Carole Cain state that "identities …do not come into being, take hold in lives, or remain vibrant without considerable work in and for the person" (vi). As these and other scholars (McBeth; Prior, "How Do"; Zittoun; Zittoun, et al.; Wang, "Becoming") have argued, much of the work of becoming involves acting with inscriptions, as inscriptions create the discursive and material spaces where people can do that work. Describing the variety of inscriptions central to his becoming as a Queer kid in rural Central Pennsylvania, the array of texts "that promised something that lied beyond my boundaries, but maybe still attainable someday" (7), McBeth writes that "early in my preadolescent life, I read (and then rewrote) the world because I felt dissatisfied with the one in which I lived; drawing, reading, writing, and viewing spurred that fantasy world which buoyed me until I could make life-changing decisions as an adult" (7). To overlook Samuel's acting with inscriptions would be to overlook the very text that allowed him to, quite literally, draw together important histories of meaning-making in ways that allowed him to assemble an identity as a veterinarian who can be a leader in his church. In this sense, Samuel's laminated trajectory as a scientist-in-the-making underscores the vitally important roles that inscriptional texts, practices, and spaces play in the complex, historical, embodied, and necessarily semiotic work of human meaning-making and becoming. The heterogeneous experiences that inscriptions pull together along Samuel's history highlight what Kevin Roozen and Joe Erickson in *Expanding Literate Landscapes* concluded based on their analysis of people's efforts to construct identities from their laminated histories with both disciplinary and vernacular literate activities: "We don't become who we are, write how we write, represent how we represent, by cutting ourselves off from all other domains of our lives and living evermore purely in some disciplinary center. We become who we are and engage in disciplinary activity by tying together and connecting all the resources we have developed in ever surer and richer ways" (Chapter 1).

Like the people in Roozen and Erickson's book, who Samuel comes to be and what he comes to know and see, and the practices that shape his knowing and seeing, all emerge from weaving together interanimating histories of acting with semiotic tools that reach across his expansive, and ever expanding, literate landscape and the many moments of his life.

Expanding our Perspectives of Writing, Learning, and Becoming

In "Transitions as Dynamic Processes" Tania Zittoun points out that throughout the lifespan, human development emerges from "the constant process people have of connecting on-going experiences with past ones and possible and future ones, thanks to internalized or surrounding semiotic means— more or less organized or complex traces of past experiences, words, languages, images and so on" (233). Understanding how to best support people's knowing and becoming, then, involves paying close, careful attention to all of the many semiotic traces, in whatever medium, people transform, coordinate, use, and recruit into fashioning their connections and the pathways those connections create. Focusing attention on only some of those traces would certainly illuminate the work those traces do and the connections they afford, but would leave blurry other traces and their work and connecting. The result would leave us with only a very partial understanding of people's ways of knowing and being and a very confusing patchwork of their pathways of knowing and becoming. In its focus on "acts of meaning making that are mediated through texts" (Witte 237), writing research has tended to overlook those texts which do not fit so comfortably within dominant notions of writing, texts which, to draw upon Medway, "do not fall neatly within a narrow definition of 'writing research' because they make use of other semiotic media as well, sometimes to the near exclusion of writing" (128). This analysis of Samuel's engagements with scientific diagrams illuminates the prominent role that such texts—the kinds of complex semiotic traces I refer to in this article as inscriptions—play in Samuel's linking together of his experiences with religious worship to those with disciplinary science in ways that have long-term consequences for his becoming as a scientist of faith.

Accounting more fully for people's engagements with inscriptions, and their roles and functions in people's lives, means finding ways of analytically untangling the wide range of texts and textualities that get collapsed into and hidden within our typical representations of "reading a book" or "writing a paper" or "taking notes" and the official texts and practices privileged by those representations. And, once those texts have come into view, it means paying attention to those texts that we see, regardless of the semiotic modes they emphasize, the sensory modalities of their use, and regardless of how comfortably they might fit, or not, with our typical ideas about writing. Informed by the theoretical foundations they work from, researchers taking up literate activity perspectives have used a number of approaches for unraveling textual action in the world. In addition to conducting practice- and process-based interviews over many years, as I did with Samuel, literate activity perspectives have benefited from having co-researchers keep logs of their activities related to particular textual engagements (Durst; Prior, *Writing/Disciplinarity*), inviting co-researchers to graphically represent their writing processes and spaces for writing (Prior and Shipka; Shipka), conducting initial literacy history interviews with co-researchers as a way of getting a sense of the breadth of their experiences with literacy (Roozen, "'Fan fic-ing'"); conducting interviews over extended periods (Fraiberg, "Pretty Bullets"), and making videorecordings of people engaged in activity (Prior, "Remaking IO"; Shivers-McNair), all of which have offered glimpses into the dense tangle of varied texts, but also other actors of the sort identified by Prior and Shipka, that get collapsed into typical representations of literacy. These kinds of methodological moves make it easier to account for the kinds of texts and types of textualities that might otherwise remain hidden in plain sight by commonplace notions about what writing looks like and what it entails.

This portrait of Samuel's engagement with disciplinary science offered here provides a glimpse of the many kinds of inscriptions tangled into those textual activities. His experiences with science certainly included many texts and activities privileged by writing studies' dominant view of that activity, including textbooks, classroom lectures, lab reports, and an undergraduate thesis. Woven into those experiences were inscriptions like those in his chemistry notebook and the many diagrams he mentioned, but also copies of the Bible (including the French translation offered to Samuel by his physics professor) and the scripture box filled with index cards containing copied Bible verses Samuel was working to memorize. Careful readers will also notice in one of the interview excerpts offered earlier Samuel's references to anime and video games in terms of how he understands molecular attacks and shifts. Other inscriptions that emerged in the data as being woven into Samuel's engagement with science (but that are not mentioned in the data excerpts offered in this article) include books of manga; a t-shirt featuring *Fullmetal Alchemist*, Samuel's favorite anime series; a copy of his Bible with marginal notes, highlighting, and underlining; notes Samuel took on the pages of the notebook he used during sermons and Bible studies; and outlines and diagrams Samuel produced and used for the Bible study meetings he led.

Beyond cataloging and examining the incredible variety of texts tangled into people's textual engagements, attending more fully to inscriptions also demands developing a sense of how people act with them in the world. Doing so entails moving beyond just examining the inscriptions themselves to examining them as "artifacts-in-activity" (Prior, "Writing, Literate" 187), as tools in use. Finding ways of getting at the actualities of how and why people act with a particular inscription can reveal a great deal. After all, inscriptions do not instantly appear fully formed in some site of engagement, and they are not inert objects. As cultural tools fashioned by human hands, inscriptions are continually coming to be throughout their histories of concrete use in and across multiple repurposings, many for which they may not have been intended and might differ from conventional or past usage by others. People's uses of inscriptions involve coupling them with other semiotic resources such as talk, gesture, movement, objects, and other inscriptions, and with other affective valences, motivations, interests, and values, and coordinating those complex intra-actions in emergent moments and across lengthy histories of performance. Getting people to talk about their actual uses of a particular inscription can illuminate much about their histories with it, the conditions under which they encountered it, how they have refashioned or "repurposed" (Prior and Shipka 215) it and to what end. Like the kinds of texts that emerge from the tangles of people's literate activities, the textual experiences people convey might trouble dominant perspectives or our own expectations and might take us beyond the borders and boundaries we assume, but it is important to look for, acknowledge, and examine those experiences, and to write them into our accounts of writing and learning.

The account of Samuel's engagement with diagrams offered here provides some insight into what can be gained by attending to people's concrete encounters with inscriptions. It was by talking with Samuel across multiple interviews about his experiences of the lectures in his science courses and looking at pages of his notebooks for those classes, and then at some of the particular diagrams that littered those pages (and having Samuel guide me through his own extensive and richly-detailed "interpretive journeys" as he explained those diagrams to me) that I finally came to understand the central importance of the diagrams and the emphasis placed on knowing how to draw them and see with them. And it was during conversations with Samuel about his use of the diagrams he encountered and drew for his science course, and the inscriptions he used for his religious worship, especially the verses on the index cards in his scripture box, that Samuel would articulate how a stick-figure representation of a cyclohexane molecule revealed to him features of God's character, and how a verse from Colossians represented to him the ordered structure of the carbon bonds in a molecule of ethane. Having taken organic chemistry as an undergraduate, although some thirty-plus years ago, I had many encounters with seeing and talking about and drawing the kinds of diagrams inscribed on the pages of Samuel's notebook. And having spent a considerable portion of my adolescence with religious worship, particularly in my family life and my schooling, I had many encounters with Bible verses, and even with the book of Colossians in particular. But even with my histories with those inscriptions, without those conversations with Samuel I would never have seen the connections between those inscriptions that were so apparent to him.

Attending closely and carefully to people's inscriptions and inscriptional practices stands to enrich and extend what we know about people's writing, learning, and becoming. For textual activities where our inquiry has been dominated by what Prior refers to as a "just writing" perspective, attention to inscriptions can illuminate the wealth of other kinds of texts and textualities at play. Situated studies of the literacy activities animating religious practice, for example, have offered fine-grained examinations of people's engagements with canonical texts and discourse and with written texts such as sermons (Moss, "Creating"; *A Community*). Attending to inscriptions could illuminate the wealth of other semiotic texts and practices shaping people's experiences with their faith. Many textual activities have gone largely unexplored, not because of a dearth of texts, but rather because those texts, like the architecture sketchbooks that Medway examines, "do not fall neatly within a narrow definition of 'writing research' because they make use of other semiotic media as well, sometimes to the near exclusion of writing" (128). Attention to inscriptions could extend our inquiry into disciplinary worlds which are rich with such texts, such as the performing arts, but have not received a great deal of attention in WAC/WID scholarship. Across all disciplines, increased attention to inscriptions offers one way for faculty to move toward "understanding much deeper and more challenging ideas about the interrelationships between students' existing knowledge or experiences and the nature, constraints, and activity systems of the writing they are asked to do" (Anson 542-543). Many kinds of workplace literate activity have likewise gone unexplored by writing research, because rather than extended prose engagement, such discourses feature the kinds of texts Mike Rose describes as exhibiting "complex symbolic fields," combining numbers, graphics, and writing "of a limited sort," animated by talk and interaction (126).

Perhaps most importantly, increased attention to inscriptions could significantly enrich and extend what we know about how people weave all of these experiences together. In helping us to gain fuller perspectives of the wealth and variety of texts and textualities that inform people's lives, increased attention to inscriptions can reveal the trajectories of meaning-making that people assemble across disciplinary, professional, community, and personal engagements, and the discursive spaces that can allow people to weave those engagements together. Without fuller attention to inscriptions, and the paths of meaning-making people build across their lifeworlds and throughout their lifespans, our accounts of how people come to know and be in the world, and of the practices people use in composing themselves and the social worlds they navigate, remain incomplete and confusing. But those humanizing accounts of literate activity, I argue, provide the foundation for designing pedagogical changes and opportunities to account for and responsively support our historical, social, and epistemological ways of becoming.

Works Cited

Anson, Chris. "The Pop Warner Chronicles: A Case Study in Contextual Adaptation and the Transfer of Writing Abilities." *College Composition and Communication,* vol. 67, no. 4, 2016, pp. 518-549.

Bakhtin, Mikhail. *Speech Genres and Other Late Essays.* Translated by Vern W. McGee, edited by Caryl Emerson and Michael Holquist, University of Texas Press, 1986.

Barad, Karen. *Meeting the Universe Halfway: Quantum Phyiscs and the Entanglement of Matter and Meaning.* Duke University Press, 2007.

Bazerman, Charles, and Paul Prior. "Introduction." *What Writing Does and How It Does It: An Introduction to Analyzing Texts and Textual Practices,* edited by Charles Bazerman and Paul Prior, Lawrence Erlbaum, 2004, pp. 1-10.

Bellwoar, Hannah. "Everyday Matters: Reception and Use as Productive Design of Health-Related Texts." *Technical Communication Quarterly,* vol. 21, no. 4, 2012, pp. 325-345.

Brandt, Deborah. "Accumulating Literacy." *College English,* vol. 57, no. 6, 1995, pp. 649-668.

Brandt, Deborah. *Literacy in American Lives.* Cambridge University Press, 2001.

Buck, Amber. "Examining Digital Literacy Practices on Social Network Sites." *Research in the Teaching of English,* vol. 47, no. 1, 2012, pp. 9-38.

Chiseri-Strater, Elizabeth. *Academic Literacies: The Public and Private Discourse of University Students.* Heinemann, 1991.

Cintron, Ralph. *Angels Town: Chero Ways, Gang Life, and the Rhetorics of Everyday.* Beacon, 1998.

Dixon, John. *Growth through English.* Oxford University Press, 1967.

Durst, Sarah. "Disciplinarity and Literate Activity in Civil and Environmental Engineering: A Lifeworld Perspective." *Written Communication,* vol. 36, no. 4, 2019, pp. 471-502.

Fraiberg, Steven. "Composition 2.0: Towards a Multilingual and Multimodal Framework." *College Composition and Communication,* vol. 62, no. 1, 2010, pp. 100-126.

—. "Pretty Bullets: Tracing Transmedia/Translingual Literacies of an Israeli Soldier across Regimes of Practice." *College Composition and Communication,* vol. 69, no. 1, 2017, pp. 87-117.

Goffman, Erving. *Forms of Talk*. University of Pennsylvania Press, 1981.

—. *Frame Analysis: An Essay on the Organization of Experience*. Harvard University Press, 1974.

Holland, Dorothy, William Lachicotte, Debra Skinner, and Carole Cain. *Identity and Agency in Cultural Worlds*. Harvard University Press, 1998.

Hutchins, Edwin. *Cognition in the Wild*. MIT Press, 1995.

Ivanic, Roz. *Writing and Identity: The Discoursal Construction of Identity in Academic Writing*. John Benjamins, 1998.

Johri, Aditya, Wolff-Michael Roth, and Barbara Olds. "The Role of Representations in Engineering Practices: Taking a Turn Toward Inscriptions." *Journal of Engineering Education,* vol. 102, 2013, pp. 2-19.

Kell, Catherine. "Literacy Practices, Text/s, and Meaning Making across Time and Space." *The Future of Literacy Studies*, edited by Michael Baynham and Mastin Prinsloo, Palgrave Macmillan, 2009, pp. 75-99.

Kell, Catherine. "Making People Happen": Materiality and Movement in Meaning-Making Trajectories. *Social Semiotics,* vol. 45, no. 2, 2015, pp. 423-445.

Kirsch, Gesa E. "Creating Spaces for Listening, Learning, and Sustaining the Inner Lives of Students." *Journal of the Assembly for Expanded Perspectives on Learning,* vol. 14, 2008-2009, pp. 56-67.

Latour, Bruno. "Drawing Things Together." *Representation in Scientific Practice*, edited by Michael Lynch and Steve Woolgar, MIT Press, 1990, pp. 19-68.

Latour, Bruno, and Steve Woolgar. *Laboratory Life: The Scientific Construction of Scientific Facts*. Sage, 1979.

Leander, Kevin, and Gail Boldt. "Rereading 'A Pedagogy of Multiliteracies': Bodies, Texts, and Emergence." *Journal of Literacy Research,* vol. 45, 2013, pp. 22-46.

Lillis, Theresa. "Ethnography as Method, Methodology, and "Deep-Theorizing": Closing the Gap between Text and Context in Academic Writing Research. *Written Communication, vol. 25, no. 3,* 2008, pp. 353-388.

Marotta, Calley. "Who Has the Right to Write? Custodian Writing and White Property in the University." *College English*, vol. 81, no. 3, 2019, pp. 163-82.

McBeth, Mark. *Queer Literacies: Discourses and Discontents*. Lexington Books, 2019.

Medway, Peter. "Fuzzy Genres and Community Identities: The Case of Architecture Students' Sketchbooks." *The Rhetoric and Ideology of Genre: Strategies for Stability and Change,* edited by Richard Coe, Loreli Lingard, and Tatiana Teslenko, Hampton Press, 2002, pp. 123-153.

Miller, Peggy, Hengst, Julie, and Wang, Su-hua. "Ethnographic Methods: Applications from Developmental Cultural Psychology." *Qualitative Research in Psychology: Expanding Perspectives in Methodology and Design*, edited by Paul M. Camic, Jean E. Rhodes, and Lucy Yardley, American Psychological Association, 2003. pp. 219-242.

Moss, Beverly. *A Community Text Arises: A Literate Text and a Literacy Tradition in African-American Churches*. Hampton, 2003.

—. "Creating a Community: Literacy Events in African American Churches." *Literacy Across Communities,* edited by Beverly J. Moss, Hampton, 1994, pp, 147-178.

Musgrove, Laurence, and Myra Musgrove. "Drawing is Learning." *Journal of the Assembly for Expanded Perspectives of Learning,* vol. 20, 2014-2015, pp. 91-102.

Ochs, Elinor, Sally Jacoby, and Patrick Gonzales. "Interpretive Journeys: How Physicists Talk and Travel through Graphic Space." *Configurations,* vol. 2, no. 1, 1994, pp. 151-171.

Pratt, Mary Louise. "Arts of the Contact Zone." *Profession,* vol. 91, 1991, pp. 33-40.

Prior, Paul. "How do Moments Add up to Lives: Trajectories of Semiotic Becoming vs. Tales of School Learning in Four Modes." *Making Future Matters,* edited by Rick Wysocki and Mary P. Sheridan, Computers and Composition Digital Press/Utah State University Press, 2018. Retrieved from http://ccdigitalpress.org/makingfuturematters.

—. "Remaking IO: Semiotic Remediation in the Design Process." *Exploring Semiotic Remediation as Discourse Practice,* edited by Paul Prior and Julie Hengst, Palgrave/Macmillan, 2010, pp. 206-234.

—. "Setting a Research Agenda for Lifespan Writing Development: The Long View from Where?" *Research in the Teaching of English,* vol. 52, no. 2, 2017, pp. 211-219.

—. "A Sociocultural Theory of Writing." *The Handbook of Writing Research,* edited by Charles MacArthur, Steve Graham, and Jill Fitzgerald, Guilford Press, 2005, pp. 54-66.

—. *Writing/disciplinarity: A Sociohistoric Account of Literate Activity in the Academy.* Erlbaum, 1998.

—. "Writing, Literate Activity, Semiotic Remediation: A Sociocultural Approach." *Writing(s) at the Crossroads: The Process/Product Interface,* edited by Georgeta Cislaru, John Benjamins, 2015. pp. 183-202.

Prior, Paul, and Jody Shipka. "Chronotopic Lamination: Tracing the Contours of Literate Activity." *Writing Selves, Writing Societies: Research from Activity Perspectives,* edited by Charles Bazerman and David R. Russell, The WAC Clearinghouse, 2003, pp. 180-238.

Roozen, Kevin. "Coming to Act with Tables: Tracing the Laminated Trajectories of an Engineer-in-the-Making**.**" *Learning, Culture, and Social Interaction.* Special Issue. *Writing Across: Tracing Transliteracies as Becoming over Time, Space, and Settings,* vol. 24, 2020, pp. 1-12.

—. "'Fan fic-ing' English Studies: A Case Study Exploring the Interplay of Vernacular Literacies and Disciplinary Engagement." *Research in the Teaching of English,* vol. 44, no. 2, 2009, pp. 136-169.

Roozen, Kevin, and Joe Erickson. *Expanding Literate Landscapes: Persons, Practices, and Sociohistoric Perspectives of Disciplinary Development.* Logan, UT. Computers and Composition Digital Press/Utah State University Press, 2017.

Rose, Mike. "Words in Action: Rethinking Workplace Literacy." *Research in the Teaching of English,* vol. 38, no. 1, 2003, pp. 125-128.

Shipka, Jody. *Toward a Composition Made Whole.* University of Pittsburgh Press, 2011.

Shivers-McNair, Ann. "Mediation and Mattering: A Case Study of Making Literacies in a Maker Space." *Language, Culture and Social Interaction,* vol. 24, 2020, pp. 12-34.

Stornaiuolo, Amy, Anna Smith, and Nathan Phillips. "Developing a Transliteracies Framework for a Connected World." *Journal of Literacy Research,* vol. 49, 2017, pp. 68-91.

Voloshinov, Valentin. *Marxism and the Philosophy of Language,* translated by Ladislav Matejka and Irwin Titunik, Harvard University Press, 1973.

Vygotsky, Lev. *Problems of General Psychology: The Collected Works of L. S. Vygotsky, Volume .*, translated by Norris Minick, Plenum, 1987.

Wang, Xiqiao. "Becoming Multilingual Writers through Translation." *Research in the Teaching of English*, vol. 54, no. 3, 2020, pp. 206-230.

—. "Tracing Connections and Disconnects: Reading, Writing, and Digital Literacies across Contexts." *College Composition and Communication,* vol. 70., no. 4, 2018, pp. 560-589.

Wertsch, James V. *Mind as Action.* Oxford University Press, 1998.

—. *Voices of the Mind: A Sociocultural Approach to Mediated Action.* Harvard University Press, 1991.

Witte, Stephen P. "Context, Text, Intertext: Toward a Constructivist Semiotic of Writing." *Written Communication, vol. 9*, no. 2, 1992, pp. 237-308.

Zittoun, Tania. "Transitions as Dynamic Processes – A Commentary." *Learning, Culture and Social Interaction,* vol. 3, 2014, pp. 232-236.

Zittoun, Tania, Jean Valsiner, Dankert Vedeler, Joao Salgado, Miguel M. Goncalves, and Dieter Ferring. *Human Development in the Lifecourse: Melodies of Living.* Cambridge, 2013.

Contemplative Correspondence and the Muscle of Metaphor: An Interview with Rev. Karen Hering

Christopher Basgier

Karen Hering, a Unitarian Universalist minister serving Unity Church-Unitarian in St. Paul, Minnesota, is author of Writing to Wake the Soul: Opening the Sacred Conversation Within. *In her book, Rev. Hering leads readers through the practice of contemplative correspondence, which she describes as "a spiritual practice of writing rooted in theology and story; drawn to the surface by questions, prompts, and ellipses; and most fully experienced when its words are accepted as invitations into conversations and relationships with others" (xx). A committed Unitarian Universalist myself, I first learned about Rev. Hering and her book from my own minister, Rev. Chris Rothbauer, after I delivered a lay-led service at Auburn Unitarian Universalist Fellowship titled "Writing as a Way of Being Human," inspired by Robert Yagelski's* Writing as a Way of Being. *I bought her book and began working my way through it, writing from its myriad prompts on topics like love, grace, and redemption.*

I was nearly finished with it when I had opportunity to interview Rev. Hering about the ways writing can serve as a meaningful contemplative practice in our present moment. We spoke via Zoom on the eve of the 2020 presidential election, she in her garret office, me in my kitchen. Our conversation ranged far, from her experiences reading while bedridden during her childhood, to the power of metaphor for expanding our spiritual purview, to the ways embodied writing can counteract the detrimental effects of whiteness.

We began our conversation with a traditional Unitarian Universalist ritual: a chalice lighting and a reading. The chalice itself symbolizes "the light of reason, the warmth of community, and the flame of hope" ("Flaming Chalice").

Christopher Basgier: I found this reading, called "Across the Distance," by Laura Thompson, and it seemed appropriate, given that we're having this conversation from half a continent away.

> Across the distance, the light from within me shines, sending love to all
> Across the distance, your light is fuel that warms me
> and helps to keep my own light burning
> Together, we keep the flame of community burning bright

I thought that was a nice one.

To start our conversation, I'm hoping you can tell me about your history as a writer. When did you first begin to see yourself as a writer? What is a significant memory you have about learning to write? When did you first come to see the potential of writing for spiritual practice?

Karen Hering: I cannot actually remember either not wanting to be or not thinking I was a writer. In my childhood, I had a number of illnesses that kept me bedridden for long periods of time. I was in grade school, and during that time, my best companions were my books. I spent a lot of time reading. I wrote to authors that I was reading, and I made a pledge to myself. I said, these books have seen me through this difficult time. If I can do the same for somebody else when I grow up, I would like to do that.

CB: Do you remember who you were reading?

KH: These were children's books, like Scott Corbett, along with a whole bunch of Caldecott winners. My perennial favorite was P.L. Travers' series of Mary Poppins books—not the Disney version of Mary Poppins, but those beautiful novels that are chock full of mythology and symbolism. Only later did I learn as an adult that Travers was quite schooled in mythology.

CB: That's a great reading-focused memory. Do you have like a distinctive memory of writing in your youth that sticks out in your mind, either in school or self-sponsored?

KH: Well, the first time my writing was recognized by somebody outside of my immediate circle was in high school when I received the writing award from the National Council of Teachers of English. It was a really big deal for me because I wrote something that was a particularly dark piece of fiction. In my own world at that time, I thought that was probably not going to be very popular, and indeed it was well received. That was the first time that I thought, oh, okay, this is something that I can do that will connect to people outside my immediate circle. I did not know published writers when I was growing up, so my imagination of what it meant to be a writer was very limited, and that early recognition was very important to me. (I'm happy that this interview might be a way of saying thank you to NCTE for its work encouraging young writers.)

CB: Can you excavate that memory or conception of what it meant to be a writer to you?

KH: I imagined it to be someone who was steeped in story as a window to the world. I could think of all of these stories that had changed my life, but to think of them as originating somewhere? I didn't know anybody who even had a home office where they would do writing. That was beyond my upbringing, so I didn't even know to imagine that. I could think of Jo in *Little Women* sitting in her little garret room. And as you can see here, I have a garret office now. So maybe that's part of it!

CB: I often talk with my students about the myth of the lone author alone in his (gender purposely identified) office, spouting genius onto the page, and how that can be such an intimidating image for writers who don't have that kind of experience, who don't have that kind of space, who don't feel like they can do that kind of "genius level" writing. It makes writing inaccessible. But it almost sounds like you didn't have that kind of intimidating conception to even block you from writing.

KH: That's a really good point because I would not have imagined writing as an academic pursuit, which already strips away that sort of ivory tower idea of it. If anything, I would have thought that it was something that somebody did in the wee hours of night processing their lived experience. That's very much how I grew into it myself. I was a journal keeper.

I remember my very first journal as a kid, writing on the very first page, "If anybody ever finds this, please, don't judge me for what is here. I'm just trying to make sense of things." I laugh at that now because that's sort of at the heart of how I open my writing sessions. I say to suspend your inner critic. This is just a conversation between you and your soul and it doesn't have to be written perfectly. I do remember writing that in my first journal, and from that point on my journals were where I went to understand what life was about and to understand my relationship to others.

CB: It's amazing to think that, even then, you were recognizing the potential for an external audience and trying to address them before you then were able to address yourself, to have that conversation with yourself.

How did you come to the work of ministry, the path of literary ministry, and Unitarian Universalism?

KH: I grew up in a conservative Christian tradition and in a very devout family. It was a big part of my upbringing. To this day, the church my family belonged to doesn't ordain women, so I had a deeply-ingrained message that ministry was not a path that was open to me, but I understood very quickly as I grew up in that tradition that not only was that path not open to me, but my whole understanding of faith was not welcome in that tradition. But over time, I learned about other perspectives, even within Christianity, that were more open. I sometimes say I was raised in the Missouri Synod Lutheran, I was educated by Jesuits at the university level, then I was deeply shaped by activism in interfaith social justice work and shaped again by going to a United Church of Christ seminary. And along the way, I was welcomed and nurtured by Unitarian Universalism that became my own faith home.

So my own life experience has made me honor what happens on the borderlands of religious life. I welcome the exchange between different communities and traditions of faith. I think we learn from one another, not only about other views, but we learn what our own view is, and we learn to recognize where they are related and where they are different.

I didn't initially think I was going to be a minister. I thought I was just going to seminary to steep my writing in theology. I still had this idea that writing had always been a spiritual practice for me, and I was going to go steep it in theology and find out what that meant. As they often say about seminary, you can only see so far down the road, and you can expect a lot of turns in the road as you follow your call. I found that to be true. I went in thinking I was getting a Masters of Theology and the Arts, and I took another turn and got a Masters of Divinity.

Then as I was pursuing ordination I realized, oh, maybe I'm not even being ordained to a congregational ministry. I'm being ordained to a literary ministry. I had a spiritual director while I was in seminary who said, "Karen maybe what you're being called to do hasn't yet been created."

And indeed, that is part of my understanding of writing as a spiritual practice, too, because the whole practice is based on offering people writing prompts that are really just unfinished sentences. It says, here's the beginning of a sentence. Take it where you will. Follow it wherever it leads you and see where you come out. That to me is where each of us is asked to go in life as well. The idea that any of our sentences are complete before we participate in them is not part of my theology and my outlook, so it made sense that I ended up making up my ministry.

CB: Can you tell me a little bit more about the development of the ministry? How did it take shape? After that moment with your spiritual director, how did you say, okay I guess I gotta figure this thing out, and then start crafting it and making it explicit?

KH: My seminary program ended with a class that was about each of us really explaining our call, and writing that out in a paper and naming how we knew that was our call to ministry. As I began writing that paper, I thought, oh, this is not congregational ministry. This is something else. I was kind of terrified in that moment because I thought, I am naming something I've never seen in practice, not in this way. It's not that I made this up whole cloth. It's based on a very long practice of creative process work with a lot of people. But I was putting it together in a new way as a ministry. I delivered my paper to the class describing a literary ministry and I thought I was at least going to be met with skepticism. Instead, they all cheered and they said, "Well, thank God you finally figured that out! We've been waiting for you to see this!"

CB: They knew before you did!

KH: Yes, yes! After that, I presented the idea to a minister who had served on our national body that approves people for ordination. I said, "Okay, so I want to be a literary minister and here's my proposal before I go to the national committee, please tell me what might be of concern to them?" He looked at it and he said, "I love this. Do you want to do this here?" That was the beginning of a long partnership with the congregation where my ministry is still rooted.

CB: When did you first hit upon the term *contemplative correspondence*, and why those two words?

KH: That naming was collaborative too. While I was working on *Writing to Wake the Soul*, I'd been leading this spiritual practice of writing for a good number of years already, but I hadn't named it yet. I just called it "open page writing" at the time. As I sat down to write a book about it, I realized I needed a name. There was another Unitarian

Universalist minister who was working on her own book at the time, and we were writing buddies. We would call each other every two weeks and name where we were in our work and what was working and what was challenging. One day I said to her, "I gotta name this. Here are a couple of options, but none of them seems right." And so we just brainstormed. Out of that brainstorming these two words surfaced as the right name.

Here's why. Because the practice is contemplative: it asks us to quiet the noise of the world for a while, to sit in the silence until we hear something that comes from our own heart and from the larger spirit of life or source of oneness that we connect to. To me, that's what contemplative practices do. They are both deeply personal listening and tremendously connected to something beyond us. The term named this as a contemplative practice, but then it also said, this is a correspondence. First of all, it's a correspondence between you and yourself, between you and your page, you and your heart. You are writing to and from yourself, so you really don't have to worry about getting it wrong. You are the speaker and the receiver, so misunderstanding should be reduced. Just let the words come how they do. It is also a correspondence between things. It's a form of writing that asks us to look at the relationship or correspondence between you and your sacred source, between you and me, between this and that, between the particular and the universal. That to me is a really important part of it because there is a lot of writing practice and creative process work that is very good in and of itself, but it's not quite as deeply stitched to something larger. For me, naming this as contemplative correspondence says, yes, this is rooted specifically in your life experience, but it is about so much more. And that "something more" is what makes it a spiritual practice.

CB: In the introduction to *Writing to Wake the Soul*, you explain that contemplative correspondence resembles a number of spiritual practices, from *lectio divina* to Tai Chi to yoga. Do you engage in any of these other practices? If so, how would you characterize the relationship between them in your life? How does that practice intersect with or supplement the writing in your life?

KH: I practice Tai Chi, and in a particular kind of Tai Chi that is taught by Chungliang Al Huang. He is the founder of the Living Tao Foundation and his form of Tai Chi is perfect for me because it's all about metaphor! He has recreated different Tai Chi forms, some based on the metaphors of the five Chinese elements.

You know, the writing practice of contemplative correspondence is all about metaphor, and a metaphor is really just a bridge between the tangible, embodied world and that "something more" beyond it. And to me, the body is the greatest metaphor. If you look at words that are especially emotionally resonant, they tend to come from our embodied experience. That is the joy of poetry. It lives in this tangible, sense-filled world of the body. As the Chinese poets say, poetry describes that material world. Then at certain point, the poet lifts their eyes to a wider horizon. I love that lifting of the eyes. You can almost hear it in a poetry reading when the poet gets to a certain line in the poem, and everybody in the room goes, *ahh*. You hear gasps. That lifting of the eyes is such an important part in writing as a spiritual practice too, because it's the moment at which we connect our own lived experience with something more universal.

That's actually also how writing can be healing. If you write about a painful experience and you never lift your eyes to something larger, there is evidence to show that you can be re-traumatized by that writing. It's when you connect it to something larger—it might be your belief in a particular god or creed or faith tradition or it might be your belief in the cosmos. Just something larger than you.

So going back to embodied practice, for me that is a way of keeping my awareness in my body in a way that opens it to what's beyond. The way that I practice Tai Chi increases my awareness of the 360 degrees in which my body always rests and moves. If I'm not doing Tai Chi, and if I'm just listening to the culture that I live in, it's very much oriented to what is right in front of me. I can forget everything that's behind me. I can have very limited peripheral vision to what's on either side. When I do an embodied practice, it reminds me that I am a 360-degree being. When I open myself to that, I open myself to an awareness of myself as being nested in a bigger relationship to the world, both to what I am able to perceive and what's beyond it.

I also have to say that embodied practice is particularly important for me as a white person because dominant white culture teaches me to live right here in my head. And this particular writing practice is about, you know, increasing the correspondence between head and heart. What holds those together, but our bodies?

Since I started doing this spiritual practice [of Tai Chi] I have dramatically increased the role of embodied practice in the writing sessions I lead. I almost always include an embodied component when I'm doing a writing session, especially if it's a longer retreat, because I've found our access to our bodies is a really important way to listen, to understand our wholeness as human beings.

CB: I definitely agree with that. I've been meditating for many years, long enough to know that I'm not very good at it! But I've settled into a pretty consistent body scan meditation, and my experience speaks to what you're saying too. It helps me recognize that I am a body, and that I'm whole and enough, just in that way. It also helps me learn to listen to my body's cues, which often mean not listening to those thoughts in my head that might be trying to lead me astray down the path of anxiety or catastrophizing.

I've been working on bringing that into the writing practice as well, trying to notice more intentionally how my body feels when I'm writing, either when I'm journaling as part of my practice or even when I'm writing for work as well. I've noticed that that helps keep me much more present and actually helps improve focus.

KH: Have you also noticed a difference in the style or content of your writing, as you've done that?

CB: Well, what I've noticed is myself slipping into actually writing about the embodied practice. It's almost a content difference, not a stylistic difference. About three or four weeks ago I got into this tangent as I was journaling. I started writing about the sensations in my hand and how it ached as I wrote. My hand, writing with the pen, was sending messages through my nerves and into my brain. I'm also processing visual information at the same time. There's a feedback loop, or you could say a correspondence, between the hand, the nerves, eyes, brain all engaged in this activity in the present moment. So I find my writing slipping into, like, here's how my body is feeling right now as I'm doing this thing, which is really interesting, too.

One of my favorite prompts that I thought was one of the better metaphors for me as a writer engaging with your book was the "land of love" prompt.[1] You know the one where you're thinking about, what does the landscape look like when you're thinking about love and relationships? I'm from Virginia Beach originally, so I used the beach, the ocean front, as the metaphor. That's very much an embodied experience for me to write because it reminds me of being a youth and growing up there having my first kiss on the beach. All of that is part of it. And then, I carried the metaphor to thinking about stormy seas or thinking about the dunes protecting what's beyond from the hurricane, the flood waters. I found in that moment of writing that it wasn't just an intellectual exercise where I was thinking about what kind of clever metaphor I could say. Instead, I found an idea that actually really speaks to me in a pretty deep way.

KH: That's great to hear. In my experience of working with people, once you open yourself to a metaphorical understanding of your life, it presents itself to you with its richness. We're so oriented toward particular kinds of metaphors that resonate with our own lived experience. The landscape is one of them. One of the things that I like to do with people is have them draw maps of the landscape they're going through as they live through change, and I ask them to playfully name the places in that terrain. It never ceases to amaze me that, when people begin to imagine what they're going through as a terrain, as a landscape, it comes to life for them and they understand it in a way that is so much more meaningful than the abstractions of saying, oh, this is a really hard time. No, I'm actually stuck in the swamps of boredom right now, or facing the canyons of despair. It opens the way to being able to understand and appreciate your own experience, which I think is really the gift of language, isn't it?

CB: We're naming the things that otherwise are ultimately one unbroken chain of sensory data. We have to put boundaries on it and name it as a thing in order to make sense of it and interact with it.

In the introduction, you write, "I've watched writers and non-writers alike gaining fluency in their own languages of faith . . . and becoming more adept at translating into and from the faith languages of others; and I have seen firsthand how this has been empowering and healing beyond anything I had expected" (xix-xx). Does a story stick out in your mind of a person you witnessed gaining this fluency, becoming empowered, or healing through writing? Why does this person's story stick out in your mind? (If you

---

1. This prompt invites writers to "[s]ketch a simple map showing the land of love you have known, or the geography of love you have not yet entered but might wish to explore," and then "consider how its characteristics have shaped your experience or understanding of love" (116).

feel okay telling somebody else's story in that way, which I also understand you might not want to do.)

KH: I can definitely share a story that is in the book, which I got permission to share from somebody in the congregation where I was working. I told everybody I was going to lead a program on brokenness. This man came to me and said, "I want to come, but I'm really nervous about it. I have so much brokenness in my life." He came to the writing session. I gave a writing prompt using these broken pocket watches. He picked one up and he just wrote and wrote in the silence. At the end of this session, I often ask people whether they want to share anything that they've written, and he completely surprised me by reading four lines from his poem. It's a beautiful poem.

He had been writing about broken relationships with his adult children, and he wrote:

> broken though this watch
> time continues measured or not
> broken though this heart
> love continues returned or not (Mikesell, qtd. in Hering 9)

He stopped in my office after the writing session. He said, "My healing has begun." It took him a whole extra year to finish that poem, so he wasn't lying. His healing had *just begun*. We know it takes a long time both to write a poem and to heal. He published it in our arts journal. I think it was the first piece of writing he had published. Then he came to read it at the annual coffee house reading. He'd never done a public reading before, and he didn't know a lot of people in the congregation. And he was so nervous about it. As soon as he read that poem, though, people came to him at the break and said, "Oh my gosh, you could have written that poem about me." It was this journey of deep pain that found its way to the page because of metaphor—and because the practice connected that pain to a larger context of meaning, the writing supported his healing. Then to have him go on and share it with others? It just kept rippling out and out.

That is the power of metaphor, and that is intended to be the language of religion, you know: the language of poetry and story that connects us to others. It's when we get stuck on religious stories as being literal that they become divisive and harmful. A metaphorical understanding of religious stories doesn't reduce their truth, but it makes room for other truths—and for the complexity of multiple perspectives.

In a world where we have so much strife around religious difference, I think it's really important that we build that muscle of metaphor. That's where I see this practice really helping people.

CB: Earlier you mentioned the risk of writing re-traumatizing if it doesn't "lift the eyes." Have you seen or experienced any other potential negative consequences that have shaped your approach to this?

KH: I think a danger with personal writing can be when it is allowed to be too small and too private. One of the most important things that I do in every writing session is to begin by asking people to agree to release their inner critic as a first step to permitting the words to move from heart to page. That inner critic is often very empowered by writing. As somebody who's always enjoyed writing, I had not realized how debilitating that inner critic can be. I think each of us practicing writing as a spiritual discipline needs to have some way of releasing that inner critic, because it's damaging to us and it's damaging to others when we project it outward as well.

Each of us can only write our own story. I mean, we can imagine our way into others' stories if we're writing fiction, or we can research our way into writing other stories as nonfiction, but for the spiritual practice of writing, we're really locating our writing in our own lives. We're centering our own lives, but in centering our own lives, we have to understand that everybody else is centering their lives. As Chimamanda Ngozi Adichie says, the danger of a single story is not that it's not true. It's that it's incomplete.[2] I think in any spiritual practice of writing, if we just do our own writing, and we tuck it in a drawer and we don't either share it directly or share its impact with other people, it gets too small.

That is also the reason why I like to quote many different voices in a guided writing session because that in itself is bouncing each of our individual stories around with others' in a larger context of lived reality. That correspondence between my inner story and all these other stories will reveal a deeper truth and a wider understanding of what it means to be human in this time.

CB: Do you have a favorite prompt that always gets you excited to use in a workshop or that you feel bears particularly interesting fruit? Or does it vary depending on who you're working with?

KH: You know, there is one prompt that I use more often than any other and it's one that I had no idea when I first did it how powerful it would be.[3] What you do is you write about something that you wish were otherwise, and you write it down on one side of a half sheet of paper. Then, you cut or tear it in half lengthwise, divided up on horizontal 8.5 x 11 sheet of paper, and you glue it down, so you have a big white space in the middle. Then you underline or circle words on either side that stand out to you for any reason. They might be things that you really appreciate or resonate with. They might be things that you really resist. You circle or underline them, and then you write something new down the middle of the page that's now broken open. Often I just say to people, start with the words, "What if…" and use as many of those words that you circled and underlined as you like, including in entirely different meanings, to write a new piece of writing down the middle that imagines a different way for this to unfold. There is something cathartic about cutting or tearing it apart.

---

2. Adichie's full quote is, "The single story creates stereotypes, and the problem with stereotypes is not that they are untrue, but that they are incomplete."

3. This prompt appears in Hering's book in the section titled "A Road Called Hope," pages 157-58.

CB: I very vividly remember I tore really slowly and really listened to it because I wanted to feel that feeling of it splitting apart. I thought that was nice.

KH: Yeah and some people will actually cut around the words so they get this squiggly line. Everybody does it differently. This gets to what you were asking about the dangers of writing: sometimes the danger of writing is that we think that because we wrote it down, that's the way it is. And I would say that's also a hazard of the culture of whiteness. The culture of whiteness teaches us to value the written word over the spoken word. The written word, then, is regarded as something calcified and permanent. Codified. This exercise reminds us that a written word is just a word that landed on paper. You can tear the story open make a new space and repurpose those words in whole new ways, and as long as we're living, the story is never finished. So there's something very liberating about it. I've had people say they took that and then later on they tore it, cut it open again, and did it again.

CB: Tell me about the process of writing the book. What was your day-to-day writing process like? How did you decide on the structure and organization? Did you take inspiration from other books as you were doing this? And also, I'm curious about the extent to which writing the book itself was a spiritual practice for you, too?

KH: As is often the case, my physical surroundings made a big difference for me. I was writing this book at a time when the street we lived on was under construction. We could no longer even drive into our own driveway. There was noise out there, and also this sense of disconnection from the larger world. We were kind of cut off. I was holed up in my home office writing. It happened to be during an earlier presidential election, and we had a volunteer campaign worker living with us, who was working horrifically long hours. He would get up early in the morning, go off to work and not come home until very late at night. I just kept saying to myself, "Well, I thought I was done writing, but he's not back yet from his campaign work. I should do a little more work on the book, too." So those things were really influential just in keeping my butt in that chair to do the work.

As far as the structure of the book goes, the book proposal I had written said that I would like to name a set number of words that are faith based words that I don't want people to abandon. Together, my publisher and I worked out which of the words I had proposed were going to make the list of ten in the book. I suppose in a sense, that part of the structure might have been influenced by somebody like Kathleen Norris, who has a book called *Amazing Grace: A Vocabulary of Faith*, in which she writes reflections about particular words, not as writing prompts but as an invitation to understand religious or theological words in the context of contemporary life.

CB: I will just say, in terms of not letting people give up certain faith terms, I was really surprised by how much I got out of the grace chapter. I consider myself fairly agnostic, fairly humanist. I take a lot of inspiration from Buddhism. Grace is not a term I usually think with, but I kept noticing all these moments of grace that I had experienced and that I continue to experience. And that was a very uplifting set of prompts to work through.

KH: I'm really glad to hear that because one of my personal goals is to let these words shine a little bit. They have depth to them. I understand the inclination to abandon them because many of them have been abused. But when we lose the word *grace*, we give up a good name for such a powerful experience.

CB: *JAEPL* readers are particularly interested in pedagogy, or philosophies and theories of teaching and learning. You've already talked a lot about several of your pedagogical practices, including bringing in objects to write from, the use of metaphor, and turning off the inner critic. Are there other elements that inform your philosophy or your theory of teaching and learning when you're facilitating workshops and retreats?

KH: I guess I would say that I am deeply committed to teaching and learning that connects the particular and the universal. That's why the physical objects are often so helpful because people go to the particular and then the metaphor just keeps opening out. In any learning situation, I like to think of each person in the setting, teacher and learner, as being their own connection between the particular and the universal. It's really important to me to connect, not just between teacher and learner, but between learner and learner and learner and teacher because in my philosophy of teaching and learning, those are just roles that we hand back and forth to each other as we share glimpses of both what makes us particular and what universal truths hold across our differences. It's really more of an ecology of learning to think of how interdependent knowledge and understanding really are, and how incomplete any knowledge is that is boxed into one particular perspective. When it is connective instead, it's so much more trustworthy.

CB: So what does that look like in practice? Because of my own whiteness and masculinity, I have to be very conscientious about not dominating the conversation in teaching situations. So I do a lot of question asking, I invite others to speak, and I try to use silence so that there's not necessarily the expectation that I'm always going to be the one doing the speaking. Do you have tools like those that you try to leverage to disrupt your power as the facilitator and get that collaborative interchange going?

KH: One of the things about this practice that serves that purpose just by definition is that I think of myself as being in service to the people who come. My job is really to line up a whole bunch of inspirational materials, almost like blotches of paint on a painter's palette. They've got a brush in hand, they've got an empty canvas, and they get to dab and do what they will with it. My job is to put as much variety out in front of them as I can.

I will also say as a white person, I was educated in a time when most of the people that I studied were white men, and North Americans at that, or Europeans. When I wrote *Writing to Wake the Soul*, I actually finished a whole draft of the manuscript and I had been trying to draw from a diversity of sources. After I had the first draft written, I made an Excel spreadsheet and I had categories for race, era, gender, different religious background, and nationalities, and I looked at everybody that I had quoted and I mapped it out and I was appalled. It was still heavily balanced toward white men from North America or Europe. Oh my gosh, I thought I had really tried! So I went back and I pulled out a bunch of references and added others in the next draft.

To me, part of quieting my voice is to notice and change the people I'm quoting and the people I'm drawing into the conversation. I'm still learning how to do it better, but I think it's a really important thing for all of us to do.

CB: It's a really big topic of conversation in academia right now, too. I'm co-authoring a piece right now and we're really thinking about who we are citing and whether we are really doing justice to their intellectual contributions, versus just kind of doing drop-in quoting. We're really trying to be very careful about that. So I think you're right. I think it's been the last six months that it's gotten much more on people's radar. It's been there in the last several years, but I think it's become imperative now.

So that actually is a nice segue to the last question: what are your thoughts about the role that contemplative correspondence or literary ministry can play in our current cultural moment when we're separated and coping with COVID-19, we have uprisings against racial injustice, climate crisis, and the looming election tomorrow? Where do you see this fitting in with that bigger picture?

KH: I think it's a really important tool for each of us to understand who we are and how we're nested in a larger context. My understanding of systemic racism is that it absolutely depends on convincing us that we are separate from one another, and that there are a whole categories of people that are not connected to other categories of people. That same philosophy also separates us from all beings in the ecological disaster we're living in. For me, learning to listen to one's heart and one's own truth and to do that in an embodied way awakens both an awareness of, and a longing for, connection. That is a key part of our humanity. We are interdependent beings. We could not be otherwise, and yet dominant white culture tells us it *is* otherwise.

We need to be able to find ways to listen to that deeper truth of our own in a way that is open to surprise and to the embodied awareness of connection. We need to understand that we cannot separate our own wellbeing from that others. To think that we can exclude somebody or oppress somebody or suffer exclusion or oppression ourselves and not feel the impact on our own wellbeing is a great falsity.

I feel like many of the troubles, and especially the polarization of our times, are based on us being out of touch with ourselves. Deep inner listening that is connective and not narcissistic is one of the most profound things that can happen to us as human beings. And the gift of language and story, as we already noted, is embedded in that connectedness. Once we have words to name our story, we want to share our story. And once we've shared our story, we want to hear somebody else's. And then there is a lively exchange that calls us back into that ecology of being.

CB: Wonderful. So much wisdom there. We could use a lot more of that today. Thank you.

Works Cited

Adichie, Chimamanda Ngozi. "The Danger of a Single Story." *TED*, July 2009, https://www.ted.com/talks/chimamanda_ngozi_adichie_the_danger_of_a_single_story?language=en.
"Flaming Chalice: Symbol of Unitarian Universalism." *Unitarian Universalist Association*, https://www.uua.org/beliefs/who-we-are/chalice.
Hering, Karen. *Writing to Wake the Soul: Opening the Sacred Conversation Within*. Atria, 2013.
Mikesell, Neil. "old man." Hering, pp. 8-9.
Thompson, Laura. "Across the Distance." *Worshipweb, Unitarian Universalist Association*, https://www.uua.org/worship/words/chalice-lighting/across-distance.
Yagelski, Robert P. *Writing as a Way of Being: Writing Instruction, Nonduality, and the Crisis of Sustainability*. Hampton Press, 2011.

Winning Hearts, Not Arguments: An Interview with Father Greg Boyle

Christopher Sean Harris and Jorge Ribeiro

Thirty-two years ago, Father Gregory Boyle of Los Angeles founded Homeboy Industries, the world's largest gang-intervention, rehabilitation, and re-entry program with goals to reduce recidivism, reduce substance abuse, improve social connectedness, improve housing safety and stability, and reunify families.[1] As the director, Boyle currently helps Homeboy Industries serve some 8,000 people each year by offering tattoo removal, workforce training, legal assistance, education, mental health, and re-entry services to often marginalized people. During the Covid-19 Pandemic, Boyle helped Homeboy Industries shift its outreach programs to address food insecurities by providing some 30,000 Homegirl Cafe meals a week to needy Angelenos.

The educational components of Homeboy Industries offered some 31,000 class sessions in 2019 and draw upon emancipatory education to help homies successfully navigate the disproportionate power structures within society. While we often overlook the value of workforce training and General Education Diplomas, they do have inherent value. In this interview on February 5th, 2021, Boyle examines the art of storytelling and how that storytelling can be a mode of healing and self-actualization for homies progressing through their programs. Ultimately, Homeboy Industries' educational offerings provide cultural capital to underserved and often ignored students, the kind that faculty sometimes claim shouldn't be in school.

On the Power of Storytelling

Storytelling drives Boyle's methodology, as his books and lectures often focus on the people he has served through Homeboy Industries. When asked about the power of storytelling, he claims, "I don't think people pay attention unless I'm telling a story," but laments that, thanks to the Covid-19 Pandemic, he has not been able to board a plane or speak to a live audience for ten months at the time of the interview. Interestingly enough, Boyle claims that "stories help heal" and the pandemic has left many hurting.

In discussing his storytelling methodology, Boyle dispenses advice for storytellers. He prefers to begin with a poem before discussing his vocation and the mission of Homeboy Industries. As he talks, he checks people's eyes. If they begin to glaze over or wander, then he tells a story or asks a homie to tell a story, which often regains the audience's attention. The art of discourse lies in the fact that "Everybody loves a story," Boyle claims, adding, "None of it is about trying to win the argument. It is about hearts." Sharing stories helps people form and strengthen communities because effective storytelling prompts rhetors to move beyond their own minds and connect with others.

---

1. Homeboy Industries serves people of all races, creeds, nationalities, sexes, and genders. Boyle lovingly refers to his clients as "Homeboys" and "Homegirls." For the purpose of inclusivity and to honor their gang-related backgrounds, in this interview, we will refer to those clients as "Homies."

On Giving Voices to those He Serves

Boyle typically takes one or two homies with him when he speaks. Additionally, he asks them to tell their own stories. Opening the discourse by inviting the subject of his vocation to participate is akin to Alex Haley's methodology in *Roots*, Boyle claims. While the audience might consider the homies the story, the homies don't see it that way. As initiates to the study of language, they don't always care about narrative structure, and they don't always immediately realize how powerful their life experiences are when shared with others. For example, at one event, a Brobdingnagian homeboy and a Lilliputian homeboy took the stage to share their stories. The larger of the two had trouble speaking as his words were evading him. As he spoke, the smaller of the two worked in earnest to fill in the gaps, offering words and phrases. This perhaps comedic episode is enlightening, according to Boyle, as these two former gangsters were helping each other navigate the world of words, not the streets. They are the accomplishment, claims Boyle.

On Writing as Healing

To show them that they are the accomplishment and that their lives are full of events worth telling about, Boyle works to help homies notice that their stories—*they*—have value for others. One example of how the homies are worthy humans came in the form of a request for a blessing, a common request. Boyle, as is his custom, was brief. "And now it's my turn," said the homie, an unheard of step. The homeboy's prayer was lengthy and florid, full of purple prose. Nonetheless, even after telling their stories or sharing their prayers, the homies don't see their weight or their impact on the audience. This homeboy started his blessing, saying "God, you fill in the gaps,", which Boyle found profound even though the homeboy wasn't aware of his brilliance. The interaction was in fact "profound, poetic, and life-affirming" because the homeboy, an inmate formerly deemed not worthy of integration into society, subconsciously proved his human value to another human.

Stories and hints of stories often surface in interactions with the homeboys. "I try to notice them. I try to listen," Boyle claims. One of those stories surfaced in the form of a homeboy who expressed regret for his life, asking Boyle why he serves and loves them. "Every day, I take myself to court and I find myself guilty," exclaimed the homeboy. "If you really knew me, it would dissuade you from loving me," he claimed. The expression of that homeboy's trauma is "profound to the first order," exclaimed Boyle. They are strangers to themselves and don't realize that their stories are valuable, that they are valuable.

"Every human is unshakably good," according to Boyle, so the mission of Homeboy Industries is not one of change but one of healing. "I told him, 'You can not be one bit better.' Am I full of it when I say that? No. That's exactly the truth, but the trick is he needs to see that, he needs to know that, he needs to discover and recognize that, and then he's good to go."

To see homies ask how they can be better humans is heartbreaking to Boyle, as he strives to help them "see, know, and discover" that they are "unshakably good." The dominant mantra is "good, better, best. Never let it rest."

Healing is more complex than recognizing stories and healing narratives, however. Boyle frames it in wholeness. The homies are working on becoming whole, according to Boyle. Someone who hates is not healthy, and thus a racist is not whole, explains Boyle. Becoming whole entails explanations, not descriptions according to Boyle. Arguing is not going to heal people, but inclusion and nonviolence will. It's important to "nurture people into nurturing" by treating all people as if they are unshakably good.

On the Transformative Nature of Education

Homeboy Industries offers emancipatory education that involves guidance in self-actualization and the examination of societal power structures, all with the aim of freeing homie students from societal bottlenecks and biases. For those pursuing education, Boyle and the staff at Homeboy Industries encourage them to never stop: "We'll keep tutoring because homeboys can always take the next step." After a GED or high school, the next step is college, and then the next step is a Master's degree, Boyle says. Homeboy Industries will make those next steps more accessible by offering housing and tutoring as well as help managing the difficulties of remote learning and the videoconferencing that comes with it.

On the Importance of Mindfulness

Managing the transition from gang life to the job force involves a great deal of stress, so mindfulness is present in nearly every element of Homeboy Industries, according to Boyle, who integrates direct and purposeful mindfulness training in addition to sneaking it into everyday interactions. "Mindfulness ought to be part of the air that everyone breathes," says Boyle. In the past, it was integrated into a brief daily morning meeting that included rituals such as singing happy birthday, daily prayer, and daily thought, but for now it's integrated into a once weekly morning videoconference. Mindfulness and meditation, however, aren't new to the homies. They coped with life behind bars and therefore had plenty of time to sit and think. Some of them have already started on the healing path.

The first 15 years or so of Homeboy Industries' existence, the organization's motto was "nothing stops a bullet like a job," Boyle notes, but that has given way to the deeper idea of healing. "Kids join gangs because of a lethal absence of hope," he says, "and because they're traumatized and have mental health issues." So in addition to supplying jobs and an education, the goal is to infuse hope. And the ultimate goal is to "enter exquisite mutuality where there's no daylight that separates us."

Selected Works Exploring Homeboy Industries and Greg Boyle

Boyle, Greg. *Barking to the Choir: The Power of Radical Kinship*. Simon & Schuster, 2018.
—. "Priest Responds To Gang Members' 'Lethal Absence Of Hope' With Jobs, and Love." *Fresh Air*, hosted and interviewed by Terry Gross, National Public Radio, 13 November 2017. Transcript.
—. *Tattoos on the Heart: The Power of Boundless Compassion*. Free Press, 2011.

—. Videoconference interview. 05 February 2021.
Fremon, Celeste. *Father Greg and the Homeboys: The Extraordinary Journey of Father Boyle and His Work with the Latino Gangs of East L.A.* Hyperion, 1995.
"Greg Boyle." *Wikipedia*, Wikipedia Foundation, 2 May 2021, https://en.wikipedia.org/wiki/Greg_Boyle.
Homeboy Industries. 2020. https://homeboyindustries.org/.
"Where homies can heal: reforming gang members." *The Economist*, vol. 402, no. 8772, 18 Feb 2012, p. 32.

ESSAYS

Memes as Means: Using Popular Culture to Enhance the Study of Literature

Pamela Hartman, Jessica Berg, Hannah Fulton, and Brandon Schuler

Abstract: *Artistic response is the process by which readers create concrete representations of their transactions with a text through artistic means, including visual arts (e.g. drawing, sculpture, and painting), drama, and music. Research has shown that artistic response helps students form meaningful relationships with texts, as it is a tool that encourages students to enter, explore, make connections, and enjoy stories and characters. In this article we describe an artistic response strategy that we developed and implemented. Recognizing that today's students often know and interact with the world through social media and memes, we draw on this cultural tool to leverage the power of this platform and its familiarity and appeal to our students.*

As current and former secondary English Language Arts (ELA) teachers, we have found that students often make meaning of texts by connecting them to other texts from the popular culture they know and value. For instance, our students frequently referred to current memes in order to draw parallels with what we were studying. This often was followed by half of the class laughing or gasping while the other half glanced around in confusion. The benefit of students making these types of connections to popular culture, in this case memes, was that students who made the connections had to explain the contexts and purposes of the memes, as well as how the memes' creators conveyed the messages. This explanation required the students to reveal their thought processes and how they made their interpretations, including how they connected the memes to the texts. In doing so, the students provided models of thinking that included levels of response ranging from visualizing the story world to making explicit connections between texts. These varying modes of response were the same ones that we want all our students to be able to use in order to become more confident and successful lifelong readers.

Transacting with Texts

According to literacy researcher and theorist Louise Rosenblatt, "the benefits of literature can emerge only from creative activity on the part of the reader himself." Through this "creative activity," the reader "transacts" with the text in order to create greater meaning. In other words, in order for this transaction to occur, the reader must actively engage with the text rather than consume it passively. Rosenblatt goes on to explain, "the text brings into the reader's consciousness certain concepts, certain sensuous experiences, certain images of things, people, actions, scenes. The special meanings and, more particularly, the submerged associations that these words have for the individual reader will largely determine what the work communicates to him" (30). Thus, the reader must actively engage with the reading process, bringing to bear their feelings, experiences, and what they "see" in order to interact meaningfully with the text and to grow from the experience both as a person and as a reader.

Other researchers have built on Rosenblatt's framework by expanding on the ways readers interact with texts and the sorts of creative activity they might use to facilitate this process. In *You Gotta BE the Book*, Jeffrey Wilhelm argues that there are ten vital and interdependent levels of response that readers use to experience, respond to, and make meaning of texts. These dimensions fall into three categories: evocative, connective, and reflective. The evocative dimension, as the name implies, involves the reader's ability to bring the story world into being—to enter and explore it, to relate to the characters, and to enjoy the story (87). Through this process, readers lay the foundation for the two higher dimensions of response in which they build upon the evocative dimension to further their literary understandings. In the connective dimension, students elaborate on the narrative and make connections to their lives. While responding in the reflective dimension, readers consider the significance of the text, look at literary conventions, examine their role as makers of meaning as they interact with both the author and the text, and evaluate the author and themselves as readers. Wilhelm emphasizes that responding at all levels is important to the development of response and literary understanding. Thus, readers must learn to engage at all levels of response to reach higher levels of thinking and literacy. We propose that artistic response strategies can facilitate meaning-making at the evocative dimension of response and lead to deeper responses in the cognitive and reflective dimensions as well.

Artistic Response

Artistic response is the process by which readers create concrete representations of their transactions with a text through artistic means, including visual arts (e.g. drawing, sculpture, and painting), drama, and music (Hartman et al. 121). Educators and scholars have found artistic response can be an effective way to teach literacy (Chicola and Smith; Grant; Holdren; Macro and Zoss; Miller and Hopper; Sidelnick and Svoboda; Sousanis; Wilhelm, *You Gotta Be*). These strategies provide opportunities for students to engage with texts and use aesthetic and narrative thinking to organize and express their learning. In doing so, students acquire new understandings and ways of thinking. For instance, drawing can help students visualize to stimulate thinking. Nick Sousanis explains, "We draw not to transcribe ideas in our heads… but to generate them in search of greater understanding" (79). According to Wilhelm, visualization is a key element of reading instruction because it "heighten[s] motivation, engagement, and enjoyment of reading… and increase[s] a reader's ability to share, critique, and revise what has been learned with others" (*Reading is Seeing* 15).

Artistic response requires an environment in which an individual student's background is acknowledged and built upon, including their knowledge, experiences, and how they know and value the world. Artistic response only works if both the students and the classroom teacher value it as a medium for constructing meaning. We must consider the background knowledge, interests, and experiences of everyone in our classrooms. Therefore, the tools that we select must be developed in our particular classroom settings so that their uses are authentic and so that students engage with and buy into their learning.

Popular Culture and Memes

For this study, we chose to draw upon popular culture, specifically memes, as an instructional tool because of the power of this medium and because of their cultural familiarity and appeal to our students. While memes have been around longer than the digital age, we recognize them now for the way they are commonly used in various online social media cultures. According to Limor Shifman, author of the book *Memes in Digital Culture*, memes are "content units that generate user-created derivatives in the form of remakes, parodies, or imitations" (73). In other words, a meme is a text that inspires the creation of other texts that follow, build upon, or parody the form of the original. Memes abound on the Internet and can last in popularity anywhere from a week to years (e.g. the distracted boyfriend meme or the grumpy cat meme), and teachers who follow the trends can use the hype and popularity of memes to their advantage in the classroom.

While scholarship abounds concerning the use of images and drawing to teach literacy, only a handful of literacy educators and researchers have advocated for the use of memes in the classroom. These reports generally describe pedagogical approaches and classroom activities rather than present research findings. For example, Lauren Harvey and Emily Palese provide a framework for teaching "critical memetic literacy," while Elena Dominguez Romero and Jelena Bobkina describe using memes to teach visual literacy to English language learners. In contrast, our approach focuses on creating juxtaposed images within the memetic structure as a tool that students can apply to better analyze and think deeply about other texts. When students make visual comparisons, and especially when they produce side-by-side images, they can become more critical in their thinking about complex concepts and texts. In order to create these juxtaposed images, students must consider the differences between their ideas to be able to represent those differences in a deliberative manner. According to Patricia Dunn, "Two juxtaposed sketches shift the focus from a simple definition of a concept to a more discerning representation of that concept in relation to another, forcing more nuanced thinking" (7). Our project uses the perspective meme, explained below, to encourage students to make these visual comparisons and to promote more complex thinking.

Perspective Meme Project

Inspired by one such meme, popularly known as "What People Think I Do/What I Really Do" from the pop culture database *Know Your Meme*, we created the Perspective Meme activity as a way for students to explore character development through artistic response. *Know Your Meme* defines the original "What People Think I Do/What I Really Do" meme as "a series of visual charts depicting a range of preconceptions associated with a particular field of occupation or expertise." This meme usually takes the form of two lines with three images in each line, for a total of six images or perspectives (see fig. 1). Each image then depicts the subject of the meme through different perspectives, such as the perspective of the subject's friends or parents. These images are accompanied by a label, stating "What [insert person] thinks I do." The final image of the meme is almost always a representation of the "reality" of the situation, accompanied by the text, "What I really do." For example, the first panel in the figure below depicts how a teacher's friend views their work; they're wearing a comfortable outfit with comfortable shoes while reading a picture book to a small group of highly engaged and seemingly culturally similar students. The next panel depicts the mother's perspective, likening their ability and knowledge to Einstein. The panels go on to depict the differing views, including those of the general society, students, and the teacher. The final panel depicts what the teacher sees as the reality of their situation. The teacher exists in a bleak world, represented by the black and white color-scheme. They are overworked and overstressed, holding their face in their hands, daunted by a stack of ungraded papers.

Figure 1.

Borrowing from both the concept and general form of this meme, our "perspective meme" activity helps students connect with a text, build on their literary knowledge, and use aesthetic and narrative thinking to organize and express their learning. We implemented this strategy with ninth-grade ELA students at a small urban school. These students were studying character development and irony while reading "The Story of an Hour" by Kate Chopin. "The Story of an Hour" follows Louise Mallard as she deals with the news, inaccurate as it turns out, that her husband has died. Louise is immediately overcome with grief and locks herself in her room. However, she gradually realizes that the death of her husband presents her with a previously unhoped for freedom, and she finds joy in this possibility. Louise leaves her room, descends the stairs, and sees her husband, alive, at the door. Her newfound joy and freedom turn to shock and perhaps despair, resulting in her death.

We chose to use the Perspective Meme because it is uniquely suited to help students address complex comprehension challenges that they may encounter when reading this story. These challenges relate to character development, underlying themes, and use of irony. Mrs. Mallard's character development is key for understanding the implications of the story, and students often miss the subtleties of the text's message when they do not fully understand Mrs. Mallard's reaction or explore her situation. The character development of Mrs. Mallard is also critical for understanding the irony of the story, which hinges on the other characters misunderstanding Mrs. Mallard and her reaction to her husband's death. Students who do not fully appreciate both Mrs. Mallard's internal struggle and the perspectives of other characters towards Mrs. Mallard will be sure to miss this irony, which also means they miss the main theme of the story relating to the historical struggles of women in the time period. Our goal, then, was to use the Perspective Meme activity to focus students' attention on these key elements of the story and their significance.

We required students' representations of their characters in their panels to be symbolic in nature rather than literal because we wanted them to think more deeply about their interpretations and in more varied ways. According to educational researchers, Ruth Crick and Kath Grushka:

> a sign or symbol can evoke complex and often culturally mediated understandings which can be both presentational and discursive. . . . Thus the association between the sign [symbol], the signified and the signifier generates endless ways of representing events, objects or concepts, or ways of creating meaning potential. (450)

Therefore, when students practice symbolic thinking, they learn to apply their personal experiences and cultural knowledge to better express their complex and growing understanding of a text. In this case, we wanted students to express their understanding of the significance of Mrs. Mallard's actions, the use of irony in the story, and the thematic elements that make the story historically significant.

During our study, we chose to have students draw their interpretations because we had limited access to photo-editing software. We concluded that the medium used to create the memes was not critical to this activity. While we understand that for many researchers, the dissemination of memes and their rhetorical power in digital contexts such as the Internet are important elements of their research on the genre (Harvey and Palese), in this case the important components of the activity are each meme's intent, structure, and form rather than the medium by which the students compose. For our purposes, we are focusing more on the power of the meme's format to support modes of thinking and to create meaning within a specific community, which in this case is the community of learners in our classroom.

We began by creating a handout with blank panels that mimicked the form of the "What People Think I Do/ What I Really Do" meme (see figure 2). Next, we asked students to use the Perspective Meme template to consider Louise, the main character, from multiple perspectives. These perspectives included what they imagined Louise's own view to be, the other story characters' view, the author's, and the student's perspective as the reader. For this report, we focused on two students, whom we will call Claire and Sara, because they were outspoken about their thought processes throughout the activity and, while each student's project was unique, Claire's and Sarah's drawings seemed to best represent the thinking of the class as whole. We also selected them because they were willing to participate and because we believed they would provide the most insight into our project (see Stake).

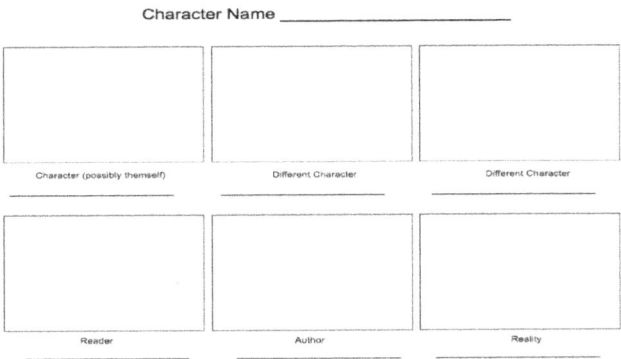

Figure 2.

Claire and Sara began the activity by first individually creating symbolic representations of Louise from her own perspective. They produced similar responses to each other for this particular panel in that they both used symbols commonly associated with femininity: a flower and a heart. In addition, they both saw Louise in connection to a man, specifically her husband. Claire illustrated a wilting flower attached to a broken chain. During the class discussion, Claire explained, "In the story, it says that [Louise] is beautiful, but she is sickly, so I drew a wilting flower. And then when her husband died, it said she felt free, so the chain is breaking" (see fig. 3).

Figure 3.

Likewise, Sara used a broken chain in her drawing, explaining, "[Louise] kind of felt like she was chained down, but then when her husband died, she felt kind of free as well. And she also had heart diseases, which made me think to draw the heart" (see fig. 4). As revealed by the students' drawings and comments, they both recognized the fragility of Louise and the power dynamics at play in her marriage. However, they did not yet challenge or complicate these ideas in their comments or drawing.

Figure 4.

Continuing with the perspective meme format, the students chose other characters by which to further analyze varying perceptions of Louise in two additional panels. For instance, Claire chose to show Louise symbolically from the viewpoint of her husband's friend, Richard (see fig. 5). During the class discussion, she explained her meme panel and provided her reasoning, saying, "I drew a person overlooking a map, like a strategy map, with people on it...because [Richard] was trying to figure out a way to tell Louise [that her husband died] without hurting her too much, and so he needs to be very strategic." She explained that Richard was dealing with a lot of pieces on the strategy map and that those pieces represented people. Claire said that the numerous pieces "added more of a challenge to his position." She also said that she felt that her connection to a less central and more obscure character, like Richard, was strengthened by using figurative imagery to depict his situation and that it helped solidify him as a meaningful part of the story. From Claire's comments, it became clear that, by performing the artistic response activity, her sense of empathy was being exercised and grew throughout this process. She was transacting more deeply with the text and engaging with characters whom she had previously not considered as pertinent. By focusing on characters that she previously might have overlooked, she was able to gain a richer understanding of the complexity of the situation and Louise's response to it.

Figure 5.

After examining other characters' viewpoints about Louise, the students were asked to consider and illustrate their own perspective of this character by drawing a symbolic representation of their thoughts, feelings, and lasting impressions in a panel. In performing this step, they focused on not only *how* they viewed the character, but also *why* they viewed her this way. When Claire worked on the Reader panel, her sole focus was on the trauma within the story and its effects on the characters. She drew "the black hole of sadness" to symbolize her personal reaction to Louise's situation (see fig. 6). She explained, "When I read the story, it feels like there's mostly nothing happy in it because she dies and the husband 'dies,' and so you're being sucked into the black hole of sadness where there's pretty much no hope." She saw the situation of the characters, including Louise, as devoid of possibility.

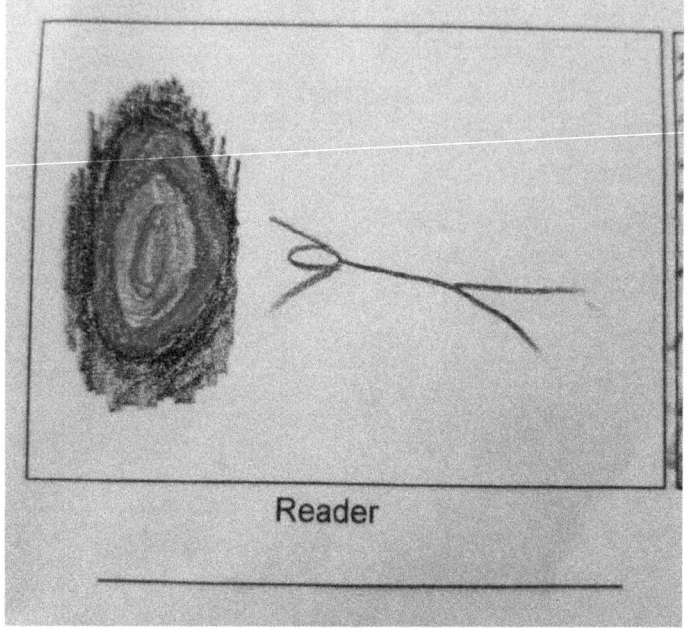

Figure 6.

In contrast to Claire's conclusion that Louise and her situation are only dark, Sara saw the character and situation as more complex and less fixed; thus, her representation of her reading was more dynamic. She explained, "I drew a face that was sad and happy, and it was split into two" (see fig. 7). She continued, "Well, it was sad, but [the situation] was kind of happy when her husband died because she wasn't tied down anymore. So, it is kind of half and half there." By creating this panel, Sara was able to recognize that there were more complex factors affecting Louise's situation, her actions, and the story's development. Therefore, the process required her to review the details of the story and her initial reaction to it. She also placed it in its historical context when she acknowledged that Louise would be free of her husband, which the character might not have been able to do unless he died. Using the meme format to guide her thinking, Sarah was able to communicate the growing depth of her understanding.

Figure 7.

For the fifth panel of the perspective meme, we required students to consider the author's purpose and perspective and to depict it. This step required a higher level of abstract thinking because it asks the students to think about and make inferences concerning authorial intent (Rabinowitz & Smith). As part of this process, students needed to consider the background knowledge that the author expected her envisioned readers to bring to the text. This knowledge included information about genre and about content, such as historical and cultural context. In this way, students were better able to consider their relationship to the author, what meaning she expected her readers to get from the text, and, ultimately, to either accept or resist this meaning.

In order to perform this activity, we provided students with information about the story's setting and historical context. Considering that the author was a woman who lived in an era when middle class women had limited autonomy, Sara was moved to depict the author's viewpoint dramatically. She symbolically represented the author panel by drawing Louise as a boat being violently tossed by a raging storm (see fig. 8). Sara said that the author depicts Louise as strong, even if it was not always obvious. However, she also argued the author sees Louise as a woman who has no control over life, consistent with the time period in which the story is set. For instance, women couldn't vote, and she didn't have the same job opportunities as her husband. "This makes her more vulnerable." She represented this vulnerability with the image of a boat, which is tossed by violent waves and is threatened by lightning that strikes nearby. The picture and explanations illustrated the student's growing understanding that, in the world depicted by the author, women were at risk regardless if they stayed with their husbands or divorced them. If women were divorced, they would be financially and socially disadvantaged. If they stayed, they risked their psychological and emotional wellbeing. This vulnerability could lead to their demise, as it did with Mrs. Mallard, since she dies at the end of the story. Sara said about the story and about her drawing, "Louise was having a hard time, just with life, and that's how I imagined the author viewing it." Besides being provided with historical background, the meme activity pushed students to deliberately consider the subtle differences among the perspectives. Thus, she was better able to understand how the author was critiquing society and women's place within that society.

Figure 8.

In the final step of the strategy, we asked students to create a panel that might symbolically represent "reality." We encouraged them to consider all the differing perspective panels at once, including those of the characters, author, and reader. Therefore, students were forced to actively engage with their reading, transacting with the story's elements and their perceptions of authorial intent. This step provided students with the possibility to "see" a new perspective where they could confront different views and choose to accept, modify, or reject them. In addition, we asked students to think about how they portrayed perspectives differently, what details they drew from, and why that might be the case. In reviewing their panels, students considered their representations and how their own thinking changed throughout the activity. In other words, they had to consider their own roles as meaning-makers in the reading process.

Claire struggled a bit with this final panel, which is understandable, as this portion of the meme requires a level of metacognition and analysis about her own thinking processes that we are still building with students. She drew a face of a woman, surrounded by question marks (see fig. 9). When asked why she represented reality this way, she said, "I drew a girl with question marks… because Louise is very conflicted. She's questioning her feelings and her emotions." Claire was unable to elaborate further. Analyzing her drawing may, however, indicate some changes in Claire's thinking. Instead of drawing a dark image, like the previous image of the black hole, she drew something completely different. While Claire struggled to orally express her thinking, she seemed to recognize that there might be more to the story, the character, and the character's motivations than she previously believed.

Figure 9.

Initially, Claire said that there was "no hope" in Louise's situation. After completing the last panel, her picture changed. It no longer focused on darkness or dark imagery. Instead, she acknowledged through her drawing her newfound uncertainty about the story's meaning and implications for the character. Claire's change in thinking may have been due to the class conversations and deeper exploration of the story's complexity, including its social and historical contexts.

While Claire seemed to demonstrate a shift in thinking with her depiction in the final panel, Sara's was more consistent with her previous interpretation of the author panel. Sara symbolically depicted reality by drawing a shade being pulled down over a sunny window (see fig. 10). The student explained, "The story is mostly sad, but there's a tiny bit of good coming through the window. Like, there's a little bit of hope shining through, but it's mostly dark." Where it would have been easy for students to recognize Chopin's story as solely tragic, Sara seemed to see it as more complex. Sara's drawings were notably influenced by more than just the events of the story. She frequently framed her comments by saying things like, "Well, in that time. . ." or by noting how things have changed. In this way, she seemed to be recognizing the historical and cultural contexts of the story and the impact that it and other events had on women's situation in society. She said the changes "gave her hope." She expressed hope by adding the light in her drawing, which seeps into the room under the room-darkening blind. In doing so, Sara challenged the acceptance of any single, simple perspective or interpretation.

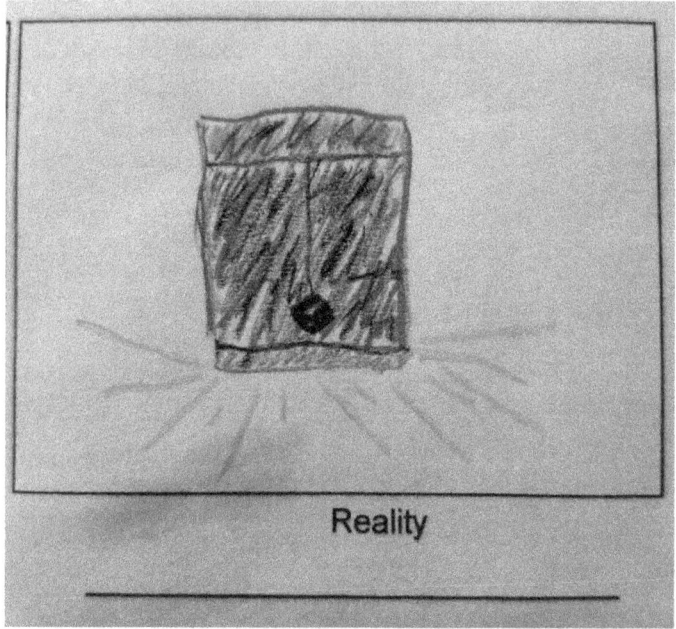

Figure 10.

After completing the activity, students used the meme they created as a whole to reflect on their own thinking, since they had concrete representations of their thoughts and how those thoughts changed as they looked at the story from different perspectives. Reflecting and discussing helped students understand how looking through different viewpoints adds complexity to their interpretations of a story. In addition, students began to better understand that it is the readers' job to attempt to construct their own informed meaning. While some students' panels contained similar images, they applied them differently and were able to demonstrate and construct a more complex understanding of the characters, the themes, and the text as a whole. Sharing their thought processes aided them in reflecting on and challenging their views. As such, this perspective meme strategy helped push students' thinking in multiple ways, not just as a visualization of their thinking, but also as a discussion tool. We, as teachers, also benefited because we saw how students progressed in their thinking while implementing this artistic response strategy. We used this knowledge to assess our students' learning and inform our instruction and to push students to think more critically using the procedural knowledge they gained through this activity. In this way, this strategy is an effective teaching tool.

Further Discussion

The perspective meme strategy can benefit students by giving them an entry point into the text and enabling them to look more closely at how different perspectives might add to, contradict, or challenge each other. The strategy also pushes students to consider their own perspective and how they experience the text. By allowing students to express their individual perspectives in figurative ways that might otherwise be difficult for them to describe through more traditional assignments, such as compositions or worksheets, we not only validate students' opinions and experiences but also help students to exert control over the strategy and the meaning-making process. In addition, the strategy teaches students the value of activating and utilizing their prior knowledge to help them transact with and comprehend the text, and it can help them retain what they have read.

Of course, there are many different types of memes that can be adapted to the ELA classroom. We chose the "What People Think I Do/What I Really Do" meme as one example of how memes can be adapted and used, and we chose this meme specifically after considering our goals for our lesson and the text we were teaching, as stated above. Adaptations of the perspective meme or other artistic responses that borrow from internet culture can share many of these benefits. In general, memes can be useful tools in the classroom when used strategically. They can help students organize complex information about literature, writing, or other aspects of language arts in a relatively low-risk and familiar way.

Another benefit to memes is that they tend to be simple and easy to reproduce. In fact, in his studies, Shifman found that simplicity is almost always a key element of memes because it allows people with different skills and interests to reproduce them quickly and easily. This simplicity refers to the construction of the meme, not the thought process behind it. For our purposes, this element of simplicity helps students move beyond any anxiety or misgivings they may have about their creative or artistic aptitudes. A meme's simplicity in form can make it more accessible for students than a traditional essay or composition, which often require students to consider elements such as organization, mechanics, grammar, flow, and style. Adding these considerations on top of the thinking we would like them to accomplish in terms of textual interpretation and analysis can distract students from the specific skills we want them to build, in our case analyzing character development and irony. The simplicity of memes can provide students a more comfortable way to think critically and to build new understandings. Furthermore, because most students are familiar with memes, the perspective meme strategy can help activate background knowledge by allowing students to apply a familiar means of interacting with information to a text. This background knowledge may include the procedural knowledge of how to read memes. However, we do not mean to imply that internet culture is synonymous with student culture. Of course, students who are not familiar with the specific aspects of internet culture that use memes may need extra support. As with all types of learning and instruction for all students, providing multiple examples of the memes being implemented and modeling the thinking behind them is an important step.

While some students are not as familiar with memes, others may have even more expertise in making memes than their teachers. This can lead to opportunities for students to show their knowledge and to take more ownership of their learning. Teachers might invite students who are familiar with memes to act as mentors or to explain how a particular meme works. Students can work together in groups to analyze the meme and how it could be applied to a particular text. Providing students with this opportunity can introduce another set of higher-order thinking skills and help students consider how to apply thinking from outside the classroom to texts inside the classroom. In this way, we can encourage students to think about the various texts they encounter in their day-to-day lives and to use these informal texts to build academic literacy, approach more complex texts in academic settings, and communicate their understanding to others.

Through the process of implementing our perspective meme strategy, we identified a few areas that warrant consideration regarding the use of memes in the classroom. These considerations can help teachers decide how to best use memes in their own classrooms, how to choose memes to fit their purposes, and how to build lessons with memes as a means of scaffolding understanding. First, adapting memes for classroom use removes them from their original context, which may decrease the interest of some students who could bristle at them being used in an inauthentic way. However, encouraging active student participation in discussing their use and deciding how they will be adapted for the lesson may help engage them with the activity. Second, it is important to follow the specific pattern and purpose of the meme so that it feels authentic. Beyond authenticity, the enjoyable factor in using memes in the classroom is that they often function as parody of the original meme. These considerations are important for teachers as they choose memes, as oftentimes understanding the context of the original meme is part of its power as a meaning-making tool. In these cases, presenting the original meme as part of the lesson and briefly describing its context is useful, as it can help students understand the structure of the meme and the point of parodying it as part of the thinking process. Third, memes are frequently funny, even if the humor is dark, and humor can increase student buy-in. Humor can be a low-risk way to encourage students to approach difficult concepts, and using humorous memes may open doors for hesitant students. Fourth, creators of memes often shed light on or make serious commentary on society and popular culture. According to Shifman, memes also make note of the integration of humor and social and political commentary. Therefore, we have the added benefit of an opportunity to bring in cross-curricular connections. For example, memes derived from current socio-political events can help students connect themes in literature to the real world.

In order to successfully implement artistic response activities, teachers need to provide an environment that fosters artistic thought. This environment includes teachers offering multiple opportunities for students to express themselves in authentic and creative ways that allow for self-expression, choice, and divergent thinking. These opportunities should be presented to students in a way that is supportive, promotes exploration, and is not high-stakes. For example, when exploring a text, teachers can provide students with a choice board, including activities such as tableaus, skits, collages, and music playlists, that meet the same objectives but give space for students to explore their ideas and further their thinking about the text in authentic ways. Teachers can use such activities for formative assessments, allowing the teacher to monitor students' progress and to adjust their instruction accordingly.

Finally, as educators, we are concerned with how this strategy meets the larger testing and curriculum goals. Our strategy allows students to apply their background knowledge and experiences to texts. In this way, they can better learn complex skills, such as seeing implied relationships, making inferences, identifying themes, recognizing a relationship between the author and reader, and supporting their arguments. Thus, artistic response strategies like our perspective meme strategy can assist students in developing the very same skills and thinking that they will be tested on *and* make literature an engaging and meaningful experience. Students can not only learn to better comprehend texts, but also to apply them to their own lives, and, as in the perspective meme strategy, they can learn skills such as empathy when they consider people and situations from multiple points of view. The perspective meme strategy is a powerful tool in the classroom, not only because it aids comprehension, but also because it encourages students to become active learners, critical thinkers, and insightful observers.

Works Cited

Chicola, Nancy A., and Barbara J. Smith. "Integrating Visual Arts into Instruction." *International Journal of Learning,* vol. 12, no. 1, 2005, pp. 167-175.

Crick, Ruth D., and Kath Grushka. "Signs, Symbols and Metaphor: Linking Self with Text in Inquiry-Based Learning." *The Curriculum Journal,* vol. 20, no. 4, 2009, pp. 447-464.

Domínguez Romero, Elena, and Jelena Bobkina. "Teaching visual literacy through memes in the language classroom." *The Image in English Language Teaching,* edited by Kieran Donaghy and Daniel Xerri, ELT Council, 2017, pp. 59-69.

Dunn, Patricia A. *Drawing Conclusions: Using Visual Thinking to Understand Complex Concepts in the Classroom.* Teachers College Press, 2021.

Grant, Audrey, Kirsten Hutchison, David Hornsby, and Sarah Brooke. "Creative Pedagogies: "Art-full" Reading and Writing." *English Teaching: Practice and Critique,* vol. 7, no. 1, 2008, pp. 57-72.

Hartman, Pamela, Jessica Berg, Brandon Schuler, and Erin Knauer. "Using Artistic Response Strategies Meaningfully in the ELA Classroom." *A Symphony of Possibilities: A Handbook for Arts Integration in Secondary English Language Arts,* edited by Katherine J. Macro and Michelle Zoss, National Council of Teachers of English, 2019, pp. 121-138.

Harvey, Lauren, and Emily Palese. "#NeverthelessMemesPersisted: Building Critical Memetic Literacy in the Classroom." *Journal of Adolescent & Adult Literacy,* vol. 62, no. 3, 2018, pp. 259-270.

Holdren, Tara S. "Using Art to Access Reading Comprehension and Critical Thinking in Adolescents." *Journal of Adolescent & Adult Literacy*, vol. 55, no. 8, 2012, pp. 692-703.

Macro, Katherine J., and Michelle Zoss, editors. *A Symphony of Possibilities: A Handbook for Arts Integration in Secondary English Language Arts.* NCTE, 2019.

Miller, Shawn R., and Peggy F. Hopper. "Supporting Reading Goals Through the Visual Arts." *Reading Improvement*, vol. 47, no. 1, 2010, pp. 3-6.

Rabinowitz, Peter J., and Michael W. Smith. *Authorizing Readers: Resistance and Respect in the Teaching of Literature.* Teachers College Press, 1998.

Rosenblatt, Louise M. *The Reader, the Text, the Poem: the Transactional Theory of the Literary Work.* Southern Illinois University Press, 1978.

Shifman, Limor. "Memes in a Digital World: Reconciling with a Conceptual Troublemaker." *Journal of Computer-Mediated Communication*, vol. 18, no. 3, 2013, pp. 362-377.

Sidelnick, Mark A., and Marti L. Svoboda. "The Bridge Between Drawing and Writing: Hannah's Story." *The Reading Teacher*, vol. 54, no. 2, 2000, pp. 174-184.

Sousanis, Nick. *Unflattening.* Harvard University Press, 2015.

Stake, Robert E. "Case Studies." *Handbook of Qualitative Research*, edited by Norman K. Denzin and Yvonna S. Lincoln, Sage Publications, 1994, pp. 236-247.

Wilhelm, Jeffery D. *Reading is Seeing: Learning to Visualize Scenes, Characters, Ideas, and Text Worlds to Improve Comprehension and Reflective Reading.* Scholastic, 2004.

—. *"You Gotta BE the Book": Teaching Engaged and Reflective Reading with Adolescents.* 2nd ed., Teachers College Press, 2016.

"The Hidden Door That Leads to Several Moments More": Finding Context for the Literacy Narrative in First Year Writing

Denise Goldman

Abstract: *The literacy narrative has emerged as a useful genre in composition pedagogy because of the perceived bridge it provides between personal narrative and academic literacy. Although there remains disagreement among practitioners with regard to its purpose and efficacy, it continues to be a staple in the writing classroom because it has the potential to help students learn analytical skills while fostering investment through the features of a personal narrative. Recent efforts in the field, especially with regard to questions of transfer of writing, have focused on the benefits of genre and community discourse analysis as a means to help students engage in critical academic analysis that will help them better understand the kind of thinking and writing required for success in the college classroom. In my work with online communities, I find that combining the literacy narrative assignment with community discourse analysis enhances the benefits of both these trajectories as students perform academic investigation of communities with which they feel a personal connection and interest.*

Introduction: Phishing for Identities

My discussion here begins with my own membership in and fascination with the community of fans of the jam band Phish, a group I have been following for almost three decades. Characterized by its extensive tour schedule, where no two shows are ever alike, the band has garnered fans and aficionados unique in their sheer dedication and interrelationship with the band. During the summer of 2017, Phish took up residency at the famed Madison Square Garden for thirteen shows, coined the Baker's Dozen, where each night was donut-themed, with playlists selected to reflect the flavor of the night. In total, the band played 237 songs with no repetitions. It was a feat that was revered even by non-fans and other musicians who were amazed at the tenacity of the band. But the fans knew that this was a thank you from "the boys" (as we call them), an appreciation for the years of dedication that they have witnessed and felt. The thirteen shows over two and a half weeks resulted in a pilgrimage to New York City, where thousands of fans of all ages took over midtown Manhattan. The experience, along with the emerging ubiquity of internet communities, resulted in the creation of "Phish Chicks," a member-only fan community of over 16,000 female fans of the band Phish. The community was established by a fan who recognized that female fans were underrepresented in the overall discourse of the Phish community and wished to connect them online.

Out of my own ethnographic research that I conducted on the Phish fan community, I developed for my first year writing course a semester-long research project that takes into account "the heterogeneous resources and social identities that students bring to schooling" (Roozen, Woodard, Kline, and Prior 205) before there is any attempt to initiate them into the discourse of higher learning. Kevin Roozen et al. also suggest that teachers' own identities play "a crucial role in shaping pedagogical practices in ways that can reconfigure student learning" (206). By showing students my own interest and research agenda on Phish fans, I hope to provide them not only with a viable mentor model but to share with them this aspect of myself, and to enact for them that "identity is located not within and determined by a particular social setting, but rather along trajectories of participation that stretch across, and thus draw together, multiple sites of engagement" (Roozen et al. 206). In this way students may discover that they comprise various discreet and overlapping identities and discourses.

What academic discourse is and how (even whether) it should be taught to students are points of contention. Doug Downs and Elizabeth Wardle posit the helpful clarification that "a *unified* academic discourse does not exist" and highlight the need to question "what students can and do transfer from one context to another" (552; emphasis added). For first year writing, Downs and Wardle suggest a curriculum that focuses on WAW, writing about writing, where students learn that "writing is conventional and context-specific rather than governed by universal rules" and "that within each disciplinary course they will need to pay close attention to what counts as appropriate for that discourse community" (559). By creating a research project that focuses on community discourse, specifically online discourse communities, I hope to cultivate students' ability to pay the kind of "close attention" that will allow them to see the multiplicity of literacies by which they are surrounded and with which they engage, and how they are already negotiators of various rhetorical conventions and contexts. Performing textual analysis of active online communities provides students an opportunity to study the organic development of discourse within a particular setting.

Online communities provide ample opportunity to participate in the discourse of one's choice and to learn how the needs and values of the community undergird effective communication within that community. For my students, I not only saw the value in working with written texts that could easily be accessed, but also in the fact that students already engage in discourse communities that fill their lives in enriching ways but may remain unrecognized by the students themselves. We desire to fit in to a group of people whom we identify with for various reasons. We unconsciously study their communicative patterns until we feel ready to use our own voices to fit in and begin to merge our identities with theirs. There is an exhilaration that comes from that acceptance because communication is life. It inspires us to think and develop as members of a society until we can recognize how we fit into the bigger society in which we reside. Once we are able to see communication as tangible, it allows us to find commonalities with other communities that may overlap with the ones we are already literate in. The act of becoming literate in these other discourse communities is achievable in part when we are able to adapt and transfer the knowledge and understanding we've already acquired. This is the goal and challenge for FYW students who are trying to find their places in a world that has just been opened to them. This is the goal and challenge also for their instructors.

In this article, I attempt to reimagine the genre of the literacy narrative, a common assignment in FYW courses, in the context of an ethnographic research assignment of an online discourse community. In order to do this, I will present research that explores the use of internet genres, situated within online communities, as a way to gain meta-awareness of disciplinary literacy. I will then make a case for placing the literacy narrative within a curriculum that supports its purpose. Finally, I will scaffold my semester-long ethnographic research project, identifying the benefits of the literacy narrative within its structure. Ultimately, I aim to propose the literacy narrative situated within community discourse as a blueprint for which students can map their own literacy acquisition of a chosen discourse, something which may aid them in the future acquisition of academic discourses as well as the discourses they will encounter in the workforce.

Internet Genres

Teaching genre awareness to FYW students helps ease them into the disciplinary writing that is required of them in college. A consideration of internet genres can shift views that have been instilled in students from a young age of genres as concrete entities. According to Janet Giltrow and Deiter Stein, "the general characteristic of Internet genres appears to be a greater fluidity and pragmatic openness. There is a constant and fast proliferation of genres—or of forms of communication that are candidates for being a genre" (9). In addition, students can access internet genres within familiar sites of activity, allowing for a connection to tangible rhetorical situations. "Internet genres, despite the global reach of the Internet, are less 'focused' and less general in the sense that their norms are of a more 'local' and of a less global nature with regard to Internet communities…whereas traditional, especially written genres, tend to have a wide range of applicability, or, at least, they have been regarded as having this wide range" (10). This aspect of particularity that Giltrow and Stein identify as an attribute of these digital genres can increase student chances of grasping the meta-awareness ideal for their college writing endeavors.

Rick Fisher defines this understanding as disciplinary literacy and suggests the use of internet genres as a practical way to emulate the expertise scholars must achieve that "requires a narrowness of scholarly focus and the adoption of certain epistemological positions" (240). He sees genre-oriented activity theory not only as a practical means for students to achieve disciplinary literacy, but also as a way to level instructor approaches to teaching genre awareness without their own disciplinary expertise narrowing their views. Because "practitioners and academics within a discipline may have competing goals, motives, and views of their work," writes Fisher, "disciplinary literacy scholarship should be lauded for promoting a view of literacy as a contextual achievement based on 'particular norms for everyday practice, conventions for communicating and representing knowledge and ideas, and ways of interacting, defending ideas, and challenging the deeply held ideas of others in the discipline'" (240). In other words, a more universal approach to the teaching of writing can be achieved by examining the fluidity of developing genres within their context; Internet genres are the key.

Internet genres, as multimodal forms of communication, represent the multi-dimensional society in which we function. They let us respond in more complex ways to myriad rhetorical situations that continue to emerge, in which social knowledge from a diverse set of participants is integrated. This directly caters to the emergence of online communities, which unite people around the world based on their shared interests. These genres reflect the diversity that exists within the communities. Katherine DeLuca's research of online fandom communities as places where "shared identities and experiences are constructed...specifically through the creation and circulation of multimodal compositions" exemplifies how powerful a tool these sites of discourse can be. While DeLuca envisions them as sites for the practice of public writing, she advocates that instructors familiarize themselves with their "potential role in the composition classroom" (75).

Online discourse communities, whether they are the basis for fandom discourse or not, present spaces where students can rhetorically analyze texts that they personally connect to. As a result, "we can foster student engagement, encouraging students to view themselves as digital citizens who contribute in meaningful, rhetorically significant ways to communities and groups through multimodal composition" (DeLuca 77). By validating the choices students already make in terms of how and where they choose to communicate, we can teach them the importance of understanding the shared identity of their audience and how discourse is directly connected to that identity. Furthermore, "beyond demonstrating how individuals creating and sharing posts maintains [sic] the group's shared identity, these composing and circulating practices also illustrate the degree to which such affinity spaces and groups and online communities promote passionate and literate engagements with topics and compositions" (DeLuca 87). In this regard, we can connect such spaces to academic communities, where the exchange of ideas takes on similar patterns of communication and is inspired through similar passions. Using online genres as sources of engagement can promote a clearer comprehension of how literacy is acquired and how it is a source of pleasure and community.

The Literacy Narrative

Often favored for its potential to bridge personal experience with college writing, the literacy narrative requires students to identify people, places, and texts that enlightened them in significant ways on the road to becoming the communicators they are today. The assignment has become useful in the first year writing class because it satisfies the requirements of some of the different schools of thought, personal and academic, that pertain to composition. The personal versus academic approach to the teaching of writing has been a debate for decades. Peter Elbow and David Bartholomae famously sparred on the topic so often that their arguments are the basis from which these debates are constructed. Bartholomae posits the mastery of academic writing as essential in order to succeed in college and sees the professor as a source for student mimicry that leads to understanding. On the other hand, Peter Elbow sees the value of personal writing to create a voice that is unique to the budding writer, fearing the distraction that focus on a larger discourse might pose to students learning to invest in and trust their own viewpoints.

The literacy narrative assignment eases the tensions of these two viewpoints. It can be seen as an assignment that echoes Elbow's desire to give students agency in their writing so that they are capable of entering an academic conversation only after their own voices have been validated. Caleb Corkery, in his research of the benefits of literacy narratives, focuses on students' confidence in their primary discourses as an essential basis for learning to write in other discourses. He sees this as particularly important to multicultural education which "promote[s] pedagogies that account for and appreciate the differences among those in the classroom" (48). When the literacy narrative is presented as an academic genre, it creates a path for students to imagine themselves as part of an academic conversation and a bridge into the kind of academic writing of which Bartholomae might approve.

The Tensions of the Literacy Narrative

The act of creating a literacy narrative is a process that intends to introduce students to more critical ways of thinking before they are expected to tackle unfamiliar texts. This segue is something of a source of tension among writing scholars who argue over how the genre should be situated within the curriculum. Rather than treating it as "'add-on' or 'optional'" for already developed curricula to "promote student agency and metacognition" (74), Anne-Marie Hall and Christopher Minnix propose centering the curriculum around the literacy narrative so the skills that are obtained from the assignment can be more thoroughly processed by students. When we view it simply as a precursor to academic writing, "the value of the literacy narrative can easily be lost when students move to assignments framed by more traditional academic genres" (58), in which they "struggle with what counts as evidence [and] how to distance themselves from text and 'feign' objectivity" (75), two skills often expected in FYW. Prioritizing the literacy narrative in the curriculum as Hall and Minnix argue for will emphasize why and how we use certain genres in certain situations. This entails teaching genre awareness as well as situating the literacy narrative into the larger academic sphere so students can see how their own ideas can fit into an academic conversation. Rather than a bridge, Hall and Minnix suggest we treat the genre as a means to "heighten students' awareness of *barriers* to academic access rather than facilitat[ing] an easy transition," (74; emphasis added) as the expectation of ease can suppress the confidence in newly-found academic communication that is meant to result from the assignment.

Genre awareness is also an important concept in discussions of WAW and the transfer question. According to Hayes et al., composition scholars have proposed the idea of teaching students *how* to recognize that writing differs from discipline to discipline, with well-defined characteristics that apply to the genres used. They see the value of writing transfer (a subset of knowledge transfer), in which writing skills acquired in one environment are adapted to another. Genres are not seen as concrete or static, but instead as fluid responses to social situations that are chosen as the most effective way to communicate to a specific audience at a specific time. The recognition of this fluidity comes from an understanding that writing is linked to the needs and behaviors of the community being written for. This is why literacy narratives must be presented as responses to rhetorical situations in contextual settings so that students can understand the functions of genre.

First year writing students come to us from countless backgrounds, each with their own notion of why and how to write. In the FYW class, students may find themselves at a crossroads, where they must alter their previous understanding of writing goals. What emerges is uncertainty; they find themselves balancing on a wobbly platform, stumbling into classes with different expectations, each one contradicting the other. Hall and Minnix's shift to center the literacy narrative as genre by emphasizing a thorough recognition of the genre's value both rhetorically and contextually gives students the tools they need to bridge the gap between their more familiar literacies and academic writing. While I support this concept, I believe that writing transfer can be better understood when students have more insight into how a community's genres are connected to the values and goals of the community. Thus, I ask students to engage in a semester-long ethnographic research of an online discourse community of their choice. While the literacy narrative is still a significant element of the course, it is situated inside the ethnography in order to contextualize the genre as a means of providing the transparency needed in qualitative research. The literacy narrative can then be seen as akin to the methods section of the ethnography. Students learn that their research cannot be taken seriously if the reader does not trust the researcher's methods and that they must be as transparent as possible in the methods section. Because they are observing a community that they are a part of already, the methods section describes how they became literate in the language of the community. The literacy narrative is then meant to give readers a full understanding of the writer's connection to the discourse community they chose to analyze. In addition, it acts as a way for students to trace their own journey into discourse literacy.

Understanding the connection between discourse and identity is at the heart of the literacy narrative. Corkery, in his research of the benefits of literacy narratives, sees this connection as vital to its purpose. He cites Wendy Hesford who "suggests that a dialogic approach to autobiographical writing can assist students 'to recognize [their] complex identity negotiations and discursive positions' [so that] the students' perceived 'real' voices emerge out of the discourse communities they are most comfortable in" (52). In other words, when students analyze a discourse that they have chosen, they can begin to see how that discourse becomes a part of their identities. Recognizing and recording the methods one uses in order to adopt a discourse of their choice is essential because the process can be repeated as the individual moves into other discourse communities whether this involves classes, jobs, or social groups. This is why I propose the genre of the literacy narrative combined with discourse analysis as a way for students to explore the journey that must be taken in order to acquire the literacy needed to effectively communicate to an audience.

Understanding the Ethnographic Research Project

In the past decade, online communities have gained prevalence in the lives of individuals who seek to enhance their identities by participating in discourse that brings them satisfaction. When students immerse themselves in discourse communities and look at communicative patterns that establish genres utilized by the group, they are "conducting primary research [on issues that interest them]" which "helps students shift their orientation to research from one of compiling facts to one of generating knowledge… [which, in turn] empowers them to write with legitimate originality and conviction" (Downs and Wardle 562). While the ethnographic research of a community of one's own choice gives students insight into the patterns of communication or genres that are most effective for the audience, it also helps them recognize the individual process by which one becomes literate in the discourse of the community and forms identity in relation to it. This furthermore reinforces the multidimensional nature of audiences, whereas audience can be as "simple" as a group of friends, and as "complicated" as an academic community.

Offering validation of the discourse communities that students are already in allows them to see that they are multiliterate, which is why I encourage them to choose communities of which they are already a part and have insider knowledge. For example, students may choose fandom communities such as a Reddit page for fans of the television show "Friends," or health and wellness communities such as a Facebook group for yoga enthusiasts. Analyzing such groups gives them a meta-awareness of the process and the devotion that is essential in order to become literate in a discourse of their choice. It also empowers them to see that although they may have difficulty adopting one academic discourse, when they are ready for one that they are truly connected to, they will put in the time and energy to fit in.

Ethnographies are used to inform others about the "lived experience or behavior of a culture…and the way in which this behavior manifests itself rhetorically" (Reiff 554). In this regard, students see the genre as a means of communicating the nuances of a culture to others who wish to have an insider view of the culture. Examples of ethnographies range from academic journal articles to general knowledge books that explore cultures that the public wishes to learn about. Parts of the ethnographic research project that are genres within themselves are the proposal, the literature review, field notes, and the methods section. To begin, students must write a proposal that outlines the reasons why they wish to explore the community. In some cases, depending on the rules of the academic community, they may be required to apply for permission to observe the communities. This requires an understanding of purpose, audience, and design as a response to a rhetorical situation, one in which they must present their intentions in order to be granted permission to proceed with research. Next, students learn how to take research articles on the topic of discourse communities and create a comprehensive summary that connects an academic "conversation" to the purpose of their own research. This is a skill that teaches them how to enter such conversations. Students then learn about field notes, another genre that requires them to see the value of communicative patterns for their own use. While field notes are generally a way for researchers to look back at their data analysis, it gives students the unique ability to view themselves as the rhetor and the audience at once. They learn how to write thick descriptions (see Geertz 3-36), as well as the purpose of these descriptions in the analysis of the community. Next, the methods section, as a form of the literacy narrative, is another genre that relies heavily on the ethos of the writer. This takes the form of a narrative, which traces the relationship to the community and how the student has come to decide what aspect of the community they decided to observe. Of course, students must also indicate the methods they used to record the data.

The use of an ethnography research project is not a new concept. Mary Jo Reiff, for example, explores it in "Accessing Communities Through the Genre of Ethnography: Exploring a Pedagogical Genre." She posits the use of the ethnography as twofold: "ethnomethodology as an academic research method and ethnography as a genre of writing that…can provide more authentic language tasks in classrooms and give students better access to contexts of language use beyond the classroom" (554). To further this notion, I see the ethnographic research project as a way to explore the genre of the ethnographic essay, which has a specific purpose in the area of research, as well as viewing the various sections of the ethnographic essay as individual genres that can be used in other scenarios. In addition, the method of ethnomethodology as a learned skill gives students the opportunity to view genres in context, so that they can "see first-hand how communities use genres to carry out social actions and agendas" (Reiff 553).

Ethnomethodology refers to the process of gathering data for the ethnography they will write. This requires students to engage in the process of genre analysis within their communities by looking at the genres used by the community and connecting them with the behavior and goals of its members. Students first begin to look for patterns in communication. These patterns may or may not be in the form of established genres. As mentioned earlier, students may find that the genres used by the community are, in fact, unique to the community. For example, in one Facebook community that a student observed, members tended to ask questions using the option of a colorful background that Facebook provides. The repetitive nature of this directed the student to categorize it as a genre. She then began to look at how the genre was connected to the goals of the community. By learning a community's language through its genres, students then have a more realistic sense of what it is to be a member of the community.

Scaffolding the Assignment

The literature review is a daunting task for a first assignment but an essential one for students to understand the concept of academic conversations. The literature review is the easiest way to approach this concept because it is a genre that can be taught as a summary of research. Within the ethnography genre, it is meant to provide an overview of the conversation that the student intends to enter. For this project, we study and use discourse community theory to learn how to write effectively for a particular audience. John Swales constructed the following criteria for a discourse community: 1) has a broadly agreed upon set of public goals; 2) uses mechanisms of intercommunication among its members; 3) uses participatory mechanisms to provide information and feedback; 4) utilizes one or more genres to communicate goals; 5) has an acquired lexis; and 6) has a threshold level of members with a suitable degree of expertise (*Genre* 24-27). Swales's focus on the concept of genre as a tool for communication allows students to gain an understanding of how the patterns of communication are established in order for the community's goals to be met.

Beginning the project with an introduction to the genre of an academic article gives students the opportunity to engage in imitation. Corkery explains that "We depend upon imitation not only in the sense that we learn from examples in context; we automatically use the language of those we engage with in order to communicate at any moment" (55). Using academic articles gives students examples of the genre that they are, in some way, trying to emulate in their ethnographic essays. They can learn about what the audience they are writing for cares about: transparency, lack of bias, language that is somewhat formal, and a clear connection to an academic conversation that has already taken place. A basic understanding of discourse community theory is essential before students attempt to enter into the academic conversation. As in all online ethnography, "an important research question [must] …be defined and…online ethnography identified as a workable method for addressing this particular question" (Skageby 411). In this case, students are asked to question how discourse communities can help them learn how to write for audience.

The language in academic articles is often overwhelming for students. I tell them that they are not required to understand everything they read, but they should get used to the format of these articles, which will help them to dissect them and learn to connect genre to rhetorical situation. I use Swales's CARS model ("Create") to show them how to break down academic articles. Although academic articles can differ in style and format, usually based on the experience of the writer, students can learn to recognize which sections to read in order to comprehend the research presented. I explain to them that an academic article most often begins with a summary of other research that has informed the present research. In order to begin their ethnographic research of online discourse communities, they must enter the conversation that already exists about the reason why discourse communities are important. I inform them that after dissecting the articles, they will write a comprehensive summary of the research, which will serve as the literature review for their ethnographic essays. I help them narrow down the overall goals of this research comprising a basis for the introduction of discourse communities: Swales gives a basic introduction to the criteria for identifying discourse communities, Paul Gee introduces the concept of literacy in discourse communities, Wardle makes the connection between discourse and identity, and Ann Johns discusses the role of authority in discourse communities. In addition, Kerry Dirk presents a digestible approach to the connection between genres and discourse communities.

This part of the project is challenging for many students, and I struggle to help them understand. I often think of the concept of audience when characterizing the class of students who have become my audience for the semester. While they share a common goal, of getting through this class with as few scars as possible, they have not yet established a common language to get them through it. It is my job to acclimate them to this language as quickly as possible. In addition, students are shy at the beginning of the semester, and it is difficult to persuade them to openly share ideas. Staring out at the blank faces of my students during the first week of the semester is a harrowing experience, and one I will never get used to. But I persist; I reach deep into my gut and try my hardest to read their facial and body language.

Being exposed to a new genre is like learning a new language, and reading strategy is important. In order to avoid the feeling of defeat that so often is the impetus for student disengagement, I tell my students that I will get them through it, using Power Point presentations for each article. I tell them to highlight what they don't understand, and jot down what they do. I assure them that I will supply all the essential concepts and that they should focus on becoming accustomed to the genre of the academic article. I also vow my support and tell them to email me if they are flailing. A few nods and gentle sighs (of relief, I hope) and I send them on their way.

We begin with the territory the writer is trying to enter. We look for the other research the writer refers to in order to decipher what that territory is. Then we look for the niche that the writer is proposing to create in that territory, and how and why they plan to do it. I choose the remaining parts of the article that are most relevant to the research they will be doing, in order to understand why scholars have focused on discourse communities when it comes to effective communication. To clarify how identity is connected to discourse, I talk about their identities as college students. For example, I say to them that before you came to college, you identified as a high school student. But since starting college, you now identify as a college student. Now, that is not just because you come to campus every day, or sit in a college classroom. You identify as a college student because you are talking or using the discourse of a college student. You talk about classes or events on campus, or about things happening in the dorms. You converse with others who are college students. The words and utterances, as well as the lexis, are all college related. As a result, you begin to identify as a college student. It is your main identification right now. After college, many people have trouble adjusting to the identity of a person living and working as a contributing member of society. That is in part because of a shift in discourse. This is one reason why many young men and women try to stay connected with college friends, or college events. They are having a hard time adjusting to their new identities. But these identities stem from the discourse that they engage in every day. At the end of the unit, I present them with their literature review assignment and explain that it will be, like the articles they have just read, the "territory" part of their own final papers.

While the students generally understand the major concepts of the articles, they struggle to piece them all together as a basis for their research, so I enforce the relationship between the articles and the thesis the students created. While I ask them to think about the importance of studying discourse communities, I also want them to think about how the scholars relay this information. The idea is a little abstract, and I find I must review this concept after each article so that they have a working thesis for the literature review.

The next part of the project entails students' observations and recordings of discourse within their own online communities. For three to four weeks, students look for patterns in communication that can be considered genres and then hypothesize the reasons why these genres developed based on the values and goals of the members of the community. As per Swales, this connects back to the goals of the community which is the reason why the community formed in the first place. While students are generally capable of finding the goals of their communities, choosing a post that exemplifies the goals, and doing a line-by-line analysis of the communication tools used to accomplish the goals, I find it useful to exemplify the process with my own research of the "Phish Chicks" community. I explain how I began by skimming through the hundreds of daily posts, saving ones that I felt were indicative of the general demographic of the participants. One of the first ones I chose asked the simple question of what do you do for a living? In real time, I witnessed the response feed fill my screen revealing composites of diverse identities; these were women who were doctors, lawyers, educators, farmers, tattoo artists, dog walkers. There were scientists and nannies, executives and students. In my thick description, I wrote that the post indicated that the shared love of music can create a community that—although with wildly different backgrounds—share a common outlook on life. A goal of the community could be seen as a space for these women to share and seek advice on personal matters, a private group where they could be anonymous or not, but where they could trust the feedback offered to them, even if it came from across the globe.

The observations and descriptions are then used as primary sources in the quest to find an acceptable way to enter the academic conversation about discourse communities. As students create their thick descriptions of the observed discourse, they relate back to the articles they read and see why an awareness of these communities is so powerful. The patterns of communication have emerged because of the rhetorical situations that demand a specific genre to satisfy all parties involved. In addition, students dig into ideas such as authoritative voices, why literacy in the discourse leads to acceptance, and how one's identity is enforced by the practice of this discourse. The power of this meta-awareness of discourse communities comes from the fact that they have been practicing these concepts all along.

For example, one student who looks at the lexicon of her yoga community sees the online community as an extension of the physical community of the yoga class. While yoga is a very individual practice, the community allows members to enforce their identities as yogis by utilizing the discourse that ties the community together. The student sees the use of words like namaste as a way to show positive vibes so that members can feel safe expressing themselves and their inner emotions. This is because members of the community value deep discussion and the use of discourse that encourages it. In addition, special words used by discourse communities enforce a level of commitment that weans out people who do not identify with the community. Another student writes about a taxidermy-enthusiast community which is often misunderstood, as many people do not understand the appeal of taxidermy. From the beginning of the semester, she voiced her hesitation with sharing because of the backlash she has received before. She echoes this sentiment when she discusses how the discourse in the community reflects the desire to clear up misconceptions about the hobby. She points out that the discourse tends to focus on positive taxidermy practices because of the shared goal of promoting such practices. As other students have also pointed out, discourse communities allow members to feel safe and as if they belong. This stake motivates the member to acquire the language used in the community.

Modeling Academic Discourse for Clarification

Throughout the project, I provide the students with excerpts from my own ethnographic writing in order to demonstrate how to present the analysis of how their communities have adopted and utilized genres based on the needs and values of the community. I give them the following set of questions which outlines the relevant information:

Guide for Findings and Analysis

1) What is one goal of the members of your community?
2) Select a post that exemplifies this goal (put it in block quotes).
3) Answer the following about the post:
   a) Does the poster use any typographical features (caps, emojis, fonts, italics,

bold, etc) to enforce his/her point? How does this help enforce the goal?

b) Does the poster use any special words (lexis) or terms that are unique to this community? How does this help enforce the goal?

c) What word choices or utterances help enforce the goal?

d) How is this post representative of other posts that you see in the community and how do they exemplify the goal?

e) How do people respond to the post? What does this tell you about the interactions in this community?

4) How does this help prove your thesis? Can you connect it to anything the scholars said?

The following excerpt is based on my observations of the emergence of specific genres that were created in the Phish Chicks community when overlaps in interests and values became apparent.

> Another goal of the members of this community is to find a place to express themselves creatively and share their Phish-related crafts. This is because many women in the group are artisans, some of whom have shops on Etsy.com, a website that allows individuals to sell their homemade goods to a wide audience. Historically, Phish shows have catered to such artisans who sell their goods in the parking lots, to customers who are attracted to a unique representation of their devotion to the band. Examples of merchandise include clothes, jewelry, and decorations for the home. At shows, fans are able to dress up in outrageous ways that are typically rejected by the dominant society. As a result, in order to maintain this identity outside of shows, they accent their wardrobe or home with symbols that are connected to the band. One iconic symbol is the red donut. This is because the drummer of the band, Jon Fishman, **wears a d**ress with red donuts during every performance. By purchasing accessories that have these symbols, fans are able to maintain a silent discourse with others who understand.
>
> While self-promotion is unacceptable in many online communities, because it is part of **this community's identity,** it is celebrated. Still, in order to counter the negative connotation of self-promotion, the women often promote themselves with giveaways. As a result, another type of genre has emerged, which falls under the category of self-promotion/giveaways.
>
> For example:
>
> Monday Giveaway! 〇🍩
>
> I'm giving away one of my tea/dish towels. Pick a number between 1-3000, BB rules; I'll pick a winner Wednesday. Winner picks which towel you want. (JMH)

Such posts are meant to promote the woman's goods by offering a free sample in a contest where the women choose a number. The poster uses the red donut emoji which has been adopted by this community to represent the Fishman donuts and gain the attention of the audience. In addition, she gives accolades to the founder of "Phish Chicks," Bethany Barker, when she writes "BB rules," something that validates the self-promotion she chooses to engage in. While there are also some women who promote their shops without offering any giveaways, the giveaway post is a genre that has taken hold of the community. In fact, on the one-year anniversary of the group's inception, a full day of giveaways flooded the discourse on the page. The women expressed gratitude for the community that had quickly become a staple in their lives, with offers of Phish-related wares with similar "pick a number" rules. Some participants got creative and asked the group to pick their favorite song or to guess the year of their first show. The giveaway genre is directly linked to the identity of the community. If we look at the rhetorical situation in which a member of the group would like to share her artistic creations with a group of women who she knows will appreciate them, she must look at the best way to appeal to them. Innately, the woman knows that consumerism is not a priority in this down-to-earth community. Yet, Phish-related products help us to present our identities to the outside world, which is why self-promotion is accepted. However, there is still an inherent understanding that this community would like to protect itself from the constant barrage of advertising that inhabits the dominant culture. As a result, the woman chooses to promote her business to an audience that rejects consumerism by giving away her goods. She understands that this audience will respond to and appreciate the ethos she has presented by visiting her online store when they are looking to purchase Phish-related goods.

Gee states that one cannot simply acquire a discourse like a secondary language without a full understanding of how the beliefs and values of the community affect the actions that are required to accompany the words. He coins this term Discourse with a capital D which reflects the "saying (writing)-doing-being-valuing combinations" that are defined by one's association with the community (278). Here, he is saying that individuals do not simply communicate within a discourse community, but they acquire a set of values that reflects the way communication occurs within the group. If individuals attempt to participate without this understanding, established members may be able to recognize it, and, as a result, alienate them. This is why literacy in a chosen discourse is required before one is fully accepted into the community.

By modelling appropriate academic discourse, students are able to emulate the style with the understanding that their own analyses represent worthy observations that deserve to be published. By giving them the questions beforehand, they are able to acquire the confidence necessary to envision their own ideas in place of my own.

Student Responses

The goal of this project is for students to begin to see the connections between goals and values of a discourse community and the genres members choose in order to express themselves effectively. In addition, I ask students to link their findings back to discourse community theory in order to prove that these connections aid in the comprehension of writing for audience. In this respect, I look for student responses that show a thoughtful and intentional look at patterns of communication that were embraced by the community. For example, one student observed a fan community for the television show "Friends" on Reddit. This show fosters a diverse community of fans, some who were not even alive when the show first aired. The student observed a genre that was embraced by members, which appropriated clips from the show in order to create new media, allowing them to take something familiar and make it their own. The videos were also humorous because members value how funny the show is and want to make other members laugh. For example, one video contained a mashup of clips from different episodes set to a backdrop of music with a synchronization that made it look realistic. The student observed that members use this genre in order to feel a sense of belonging while having a positive impact on the community, which enforces the goal of people coming together to discuss their common interests. She was able to make the connection to Wardle who says, "Individuals need to find ways to engage in their communities which includes seeing their own contributions as meaningful and compatible with others. This entails formulating or modifying an identity. It is not simply a matter of learning new skills, but also fielding new calls for identity construction" (4). The student presents an understanding of how discourse communities often alter genres to match the needs of the community. She recognizes that people join communities to connect with others through a special language. Once this language is adopted masterfully, the member can begin to have an influence on the community, something that brings great satisfaction.

The Literacy Narrative, Revisited

The final part of the ethnographic paper is the methods section that is presented as the genre of the literacy narrative. While traditionally this is where the methods used for research are indicated, the goal here is to present the writer as a credible researcher by using transparency as the key to credibility. I ask students to show that their research was conducted to try to minimize or otherwise account for potential bias in their descriptions. Presented in the form of the literacy narrative, students are able to explore the process they took to become literate in the discourse of their community. The result yields the same goal of being transparent and thus credible to the audience. In addition, students have fun recalling the ways they were introduced to the community and write creatively to express this.

The notion of including the literacy narrative within a context that supports its rhetorical purpose echoes Hall and Minnix's decision to alter their curriculum in order to support the genre. Their research "illustrate[s] that the power of literacy narratives is constrained and fostered by the spaces of their circulation and reception" (64). In this regard, the ethnographic essay supports the need for the transparency of the student ethnographer in order to make an argument for the importance of looking at discourse communities when learning to write for audience. Student understanding of the narrative's purpose is essential when "developing opportunities for students to 'link' the literacy narrative to their work in other academic genres and use their literacy narratives to critically examine and even challenge academic discourse" (65). In other words, with this project, students are able to gain a metacognitive understanding of discourse acquisition by analyzing their own experience with a discourse that they have a stake in.

This gives them the freedom to approach discourse without the daunting requirements imposed on them in academia.

In my instructions for the narrative, I require the use of at least three vignettes (short, vivid descriptions) that tell the story of how the student learned the language of their community. To help them, I ask them questions such as the following: Can you recall a person or an activity that aided in your adoption of the special discourse of the community? How did participation in the online community help you to become more literate in the discourse? Can you clarify how this experience helped you to become more literate in the discourse? The final paragraph of the literacy narrative focuses on the methods they used this semester to observe the community. While the vignettes show the reader that they have extensive experience in the community, the final paragraph tells the reader how they shifted from member to researcher. They should say how long they observed the community, how often they observed the community, and how they chose the posts to analyze (the most likes, the most comments, at random…). This paragraph is important, not only because it reflects the more traditional way to write a methods section for an ethnographic research paper, but also because it helps student recognize how their understanding of the discourse of the community was altered when they began to formally observe it. In essence, the placement of the narrative within the ethnographic research paper enforces the rhetorical situation for which the literacy narrative is the logical genre.

Conclusion

With online discourse communities being so prevalent in our lives, it makes sense to utilize their commonalities to teach students how to write for audience. Within their academic careers and beyond, students will encounter discourse communities that they have a strong desire to be a part of. Although many may not be academic, there is value in analyzing how discourse is connected to goals and values, and how genres are created as a result. In addition, using the genre of the literacy narrative to trace one's literacy acquisition aids in their ability to repeat the process. The goal is for students to feel empowered enough by their intricate knowledge of the discourses they have analyzed to join an academic conversation. The discourse then can be seen as a tool for entrance into a community where being part of a conversation requires research of the accepted forms of communication. If the connection between these communities and the academic ones they will be required to understand is consistently enforced, students walk away from the class understanding what is required of them, not only in their classes, but in the communication that they wish to be a part of in other aspects of their lives.

Works Cited

Corkery, Caleb. "Literacy Narratives and Confidence Building in the Writing Classroom." *Journal of Basic Writing,* vol. 24, no. 1, 2005, pp. 48-67.

DeLuca, Katherine. "Shared passions, Shared Compositions: Online Fandom Communities and Affinity Groups as Sites for Public Writing Pedagogy." *Computers and Composition,* vol. 47, 2018, pp. 75-92.

Dirk, Kerry. "Navigating Genres." *Writing Spaces: Readings on Writing*, volume 1, edited by Charles Lowe and Pavel Zemliansky, Parlor Press, 2010, pp. 249-262.

Downs, Doug, and Wardle, Elizabeth. "Teaching about Writing, Righting Misconceptions: (re)envisioning 'First-Year Composition' as 'Introduction to Writing Studies.'" *College Composition and Communication,* vol. 58, no. 4, 2007, pp. 552-584.

Driscoll, Dana Lynn, Joseph Pazsek, Gwen Gorzelsky, Carol L. Hayes, and Edmund Jones. "Genre Knowledge and Writing Development: Results From the Writing Transfer Project." *Written Communication,* vol. 37, no. 1, 2020, pp. 69-103.

Fisher, Rick. "Reconciling Disciplinary Literacy Perspectives with Genre-Oriented Activity Theory: Toward a Fuller Synthesis of Traditions." *Reading Research Quarterly,* vol. 54, no. 2, 2018, pp. 237-251.

Gee, James Paul. "Literacy, Discourse, and Linguistics: Introduction." Wardle and Downs, pp. 274-295.

Geertz, Clifford. *The Interpretation of Cultures*, Basic Books, 1973.

Giltrow, Janet, and Dieter Stein. "Genres in the Internet: Innovation, Evolution, and Genre Theory." *Genres in the Internet: Issues in the Theory of Genre*, edited by Janet Giltrow and Dieter Stein, John Benjamins Publishing Company, 2009, pp. 1-26.

Hall, Anne-Marie, and Christopher Minnix. "Beyond the Bridge Metaphor: Rethinking the Place of the Literacy Narrative in the Basic Writing Curriculum." *Journal of Basic Writing,* vol. 31, no. 2, 2012, pp. 57-82.

Hayes, Hogan, Dana R. Ferris, and Carl Whithouse. "Dynamic Transfer in First-Year Writing and 'Writing in the Disciplines' Setting." *Critical Transitions: Writing and the Question of Transfer,* edited by Chris M. Anderson and Jessie L. Moore, WAC Clearinghouse, 2017, pp. 181-213.

Johns, Ann M. "Discourse Communities and Communities of Practice: Membership, Conflict, and Diversity." Wardle and Downs, pp. 319-341.

Reiff, Mary Jo. "Accessing Communities Through the Genre of Ethnography: Exploring a Pedagogical Genre." *College English,* vol. 65, no. 5, 2003, pp. 553-557.

Roozen, Kevin, Rebecca Woodard, Sonia Kline, and Paul Prior. "The Transformative Potential of Laminating Trajectories: Three Teachers' Developing Pedagogical Practices and Identities." *Working with Academic Literacies: Case Studies Towards Transformative Practice,* edited by Theresa Lillis, Kathy Harrington, Mary R. Lea, and Sally Mitchell, Parlor Press, 2015, pp. 205-215.

Skageby, Jorgen. "Online Ethnographic Methods: Towards a Qualitative Understanding of Virtual Community Practices." *From Handbook of Research on Methods and Techniques for Studying Virtual Communities: Paradigms and Phenomena,* edited by Ben Kei Daniel, IGI Global, 2010, pp. 410-428.

Swales, John. *Genre Analysis: English in Academic and Research Settings*. Cambridge UP, 1990.

Swales, John. "'Create a Research Space' (CARS) Model of Research Introductions." Wardle and Downs, pp. 6-8.

Wardle, Elizabeth. "Identity, Authority, and Learning to Write in New Workplaces." Wardle and Downs, pp. 407-424.

Wardle, Elizabeth and Downs, Doug, editors. *Writing About Writing*. 3rd ed., Bedford/St Martin's, 2017.

CONNECTING

Responding Together and the Roots of Resilience

Christy I. Wenger

As 2020 came to a close, the promise and hope of a new year felt tangible. Professionally and personally, the past year was challenging for me, as it was for so many other academics—especially academic mothers who found the pandemic shattering any tenuous attempt at work/life balance they had previously struggled to establish. My struggle is validated by news reports warning that working mothers enduring the pandemic are at their "breaking points" and are under unprecedented pressure "just trying to make it all work…[with] no social safety net to catch them" (Pearson). This year was not about balance so much as it was about doing everything at once and under a cloud of constant worry as I was "trying to make it work." I learned how to guide my five- and seven- year-old children through virtual school from the dining room table while simultaneously running my writing program and teaching my own college classes at that same table. Like many others, I mastered new teaching technologies this year on a dime; racing since March to learn Slack so my students could build community even if we were virtual; using Flipgrid for the first time so we could create meaningful class discussion even if some of my students couldn't login consistently at a specific time for class; experimenting with new-to-me audio recording and video editing programs that would allow my students to hear and see me even if we couldn't occupy the same space together on campus.

And Zoom. Of course, so much Zoom.

And for each new program I learned, my students learned it too, rolling with the changing landscape of higher education and doing so with grace and dexterity. Recently, I laughed as I helped my seven-year-old with her "technology" homework because wasn't it all technology homework these days? The fact that her day is punctuated with Microsoft Teams meetings with her teacher and classmates, SeeSaw work on her iPad to complete her homework and countless other apps in between seems to invalidate the need for a separate "technology" class. Though, if she needed one, it would easily come in the form of helping her pre-K sister navigate her Google Classroom, which, of course, has its own suite of entirely different programs we've all had to learn so they can help each other when I'm teaching or unavailable. We've struggled, for sure, while making it work, but we also persevered. Through it all, I was resilient, my kids were resilient, my students were resilient. WE were resilient together.

That's the thing about resilience that we often get wrong. We tend to think of resilience as the property of the individual working alone. Heroic and independent and rising above the challenges of life. But resilience is better understood in terms similar to those we've used about the pandemic itself. The pandemic has reminded us that we are dependent on each other and that we are only as strong as our community. Think about the rhetorics of mask wearing during the pandemic: we mask up to help protect those around us, and in so doing, hope they return the favor since our personal health and safety are dependent just as much on their actions as our own. We depend on each other; our lives are linked to those around us. While resilience has been ever-present (just ask a working parent), the pandemic has cracked it open for a better view, one informed by this transformative realization of the "we" resilience rests upon.

Resilience is born from the challenges we face as individuals. It "suggests attention to choices made in the face of difficult and even impossible challenges," note Elizabeth A. Flynn, Patricia Sotirin, and Ann Brady in their study of resilience for feminist writing scholars (1). But resilience takes root from the ways we face those challenges together. Resilience is "not a state of being but a process of rhetorically engaging with material circumstances and situational exigencies . . . not as a quality of the heroic individual but as always relational" (7). Our resilient responses are dependent on each other; I can be a resilient teacher by learning new, interactive digital platforms and programs for my classes, but the limits of that resilience are the ways my students engage those programs and face our challenges as a learning community together with me on new platforms. I can be a resilient mother by juggling the seemingly endless demands on my time as I care for my kids, work from home and oversee their virtual learning, but the limits of my resilience are the ways my kids join me to face our challenges together and find new opportunities as a family to live and learn together.

Resilience provides us agency because it allows us a new response not because it denies the need for one, as the heroic narrative of "conquering our limits" and "rising above" traditionally suggests. Resilience is a powerful feminist action because it transforms the "way a life is lived," not necessarily the material circumstances of that life. My students, my family, and I were resilient because we actively chose to stand together and change our actions and habits to work with our challenges. The center of those challenges was, of course, the pandemic itself, which is not so easily conquered by grand individual action. Instead, we were resilient because we worked together to transform the day-to-day actions of our lives, to find new perspective in those actions. We exercised the "ongoing responsiveness" that Flynn et al. claim to be the hallmark of resilience (7). This responsiveness illustrates how resilience is a process, not a product, repeated over and over and collectively achieved as opposed to being solely a property of a single individual. Resilience changes the ways we respond to our environments and the people within them; it is itself a result of relationality and not borne from the individual but instead from the collective.

I've long been interested in Flynn et al.'s notions of resilience and how they could transform our academic work cultures and help us bring attention to emotional labor and communal well-being within those cultures. While resilience is especially illustrated in many of our pandemic pedagogies, adopted to respond to the situational exigencies of COVID, resilience has always been at work in academic cultures, though it is often overlooked—often residing as it does in the margins of our workspaces. Understanding how we work together to bring about and maintain resilience replaces the individualist narratives of the academy and opens the door for a larger discussion about the relational ecology of our workplaces, an ecology that defines how and to what ends emotional labor is attended and the ways we understand our well-being as teachers and academics as connected to our students, our colleges and our colleagues. Both essays in this section of "Connecting" demonstrate how we might begin to voice our resilient ecologies at work. While they do not mention this term, both essays demonstrate the authors' resilience as ongoing responsiveness to their material circumstances. Both essays reveal how their authors are motivated by a shared, underlying purpose to find meaningful, relational connections with fellow academic colleagues as well as with students, connections that will help them live well within the spaces of their work and attend to the well-being of others who are impacted by their actions. Both reveal the emotional labor involved when their values don't quite align with what is expected of them in their workplaces. Notable too is that both essays are penned by female academics who are working still within the margins of their academic workplaces based on their interests and identifications which diverge from the mainstream.

Sarah Heidebrink-Bruno's essay reflects on being a first-generation graduate student who is slowly coming to terms with her working-class background as she takes on the task of writing her dissertation's acknowledgement page. Heidebrink-Bruno's resilience leads her to acceptance of and gratitude for her family despite their trouble in recognizing her new identifications as a scholar and an academic. Her reflection illustrates her resilience by providing snapshots of how she has worked to bridge her dual citizenships in both her blue-collar family and her white-collar academic workspace; these snapshots flood me with memories of a similar struggle of identifications I too had as a working-class graduate student embarking on a lifetime of knowledge work.

Heidebrink-Bruno recounts the emotional labor involved in finding herself reborn in the challenging but rewarding world of graduate school, where she could leverage her love of writing and reading and her humble upbringing to help other working-class college students validate their experiences and find new ones through challenging texts, like she did. Importantly, the emotional resilience she demonstrates to "come out" as working class to her peers and mentors in graduate school, many of whom had more affluent upbringings, is relational, connected to the networks of family and friends that brought her to graduate school and the networks of colleagues and mentors who helped her navigate through school as a first-generation student.

Next up, Ellen Scheible's piece, "Collaborative Writing for Publication in Undergraduate Literature Seminars," exhibits her pedagogical resilience. Schieble rallies against typical pursuits to strengthen our majors' individual writing skills. Swimming against the trend of typical capstone classes that ask students to create publishable work on their own, she develops a course for seniors built on a collaborative, critical essay students must approach together while engaging in a collaborative writing process steeped in peer review and workshops. Schieble recounts feeling like a stranger in strange lands because of her commitment to the collaborative, something her fellow humanities faculty do not value—because in large part, they are not taught to and are instead validated by an individualist system of promotion, tenure, and publication. And so the cycle continues.

Schieble attempts to break this cycle but faces significant challenges along the way, including student resistance to collaborative writing, a lack of model pedagogy for her class, and power imbalances between her and her student writers, making it hard for her to collaboratively write with her students even if she can still guide their collaborative writing. Like Heidebrink-Bruno's, Schieble's resilience reveals the power of her community in the end: she finds value in the community created in her class and the sense of belonging that collaborative writing fosters among her students.

Finally, two poems round out this issue's "Connecting" with the work of Naomi Gades and Paul M. Puccio. Gades's tongue-in-cheek poem about plagiarism reminds us that there is always time for humor when placing the individual amongst her community, especially when she forgets to cite that community in her writing. And Puccio's reflection on the passing year through poetic allusion is a fitting tribute to our resilience and our humanity.

One day, the pandemic will end, but what hopefully will remain is that forged resilience. Let us hope we remember, as Katy Butler notes, that "resilience…is the outward and visible sign of a web of relationships and experiences that teach people mastery, doggedness, love, moral courage and hope (qtd. in Flynn et al. 6). In our haste to return to life as "normal," our pre-crisis state, let us not squander the opportunity to continue to recognize the relationships that root our resilience and to find our purpose with and through our communities.

Works Cited

Flynn, Elizabeth A., Patricia Sotirin, and Ann Brady. "Introduction: Feminist Rhetorical Resilience—Possibilities and Impossibilities." *Feminist Rhetorical Resilience*. Eds. Elizabeth A. Flynn, Patricia Sotirin, and Ann Brady. UP of Colorado, 2012, pp. 1–29.

Pearson, Catherine. Millennial Moms Have Been Driven to their Breaking Point. HuffPost. Jan 22, 2021. https://www.huffpost.com/entry/millennial-moms-pandemic-stress_l_600ae2b2c5b6a46978d09117. Accessed 1 February 2021.

Reflections from a Working Class, First-Generation Almost-Graduate

Sarah Heidebrink-Bruno

Amidst my seemingly endless doomscrolling on Facebook the other day, I was delighted to see some good news: my advisor's latest book was recently published and available to the public. Having spent the better part of a decade writing and revising her manuscript, she thanked a plethora of people for helping her work through the arduous process, including her mother, who read through every draft. As I read these words in her acknowledgements, I was struck by the differences in our realities. As hard as I tried to imagine it, I could not see either of my parents reading through and commenting on my writing, let alone my entire dissertation or a future manuscript. Like so many parts of my experiences in higher-ed as a first-generation college and now graduate student, my research does not easily fit into my parents' world.

This used to be a source of pain for me, although with each new layer of credentials, I've developed a pretty tough skin. It no longer shames me to "come out" as working class to my mentors and peers. What I once saw as a lack, I now see as a strength—I can understand and empathize with my fellow first-generation students in a way that my more financially and academically privileged colleagues might not. I can anticipate some of the unspoken resources that my students or colleagues might need and gently guide them to the offices who are equipped to help. Importantly, I can break down the stigma and shame for them so that they do not need to go through the same struggles that I went through when I entered higher education. Often, I find that I am the one called upon in my department to reach out and welcome incoming first-generation graduate students and offer them advice, based on my perceived successes. So by all accounts, I should be used to this by now.

But every so often, a moment (like the one above) occurs where I experience a tinge of sadness—a sense of not being fully seen and understood by those who once knew me best. In "Coming Out as Working Class," writer Justin Quarry recalls that, "being the first person in my family to eventually finish college, and one of only a few of us to leave Arkansas, I'd now transformed myself into an alien among even my own people." I see echoes of my own experiences in Quarry's disclosure. Is there a word to describe being a beloved member of a family, but also being an alien among my people?

As I near the end of my dissertation, I find myself writing and re-writing my own acknowledgements page. It's my go-to task when the rest of the process feels too overwhelming and discouraging. It is currently four, single-spaced pages: long and growing. I thank every person who has touched my life in both seemingly minute and profound ways over the past ten years. Although I find this task cathartic, I struggle to write an adequate dedication to my family. How can I distill the past thirty-odd years down into a few lines at the front of a manuscript that they will likely never read? The words get stuck in a bottleneck between my brain and my fingers.

I was recently chatting with a family member about his new career move, which naturally led to a discussion of my own job search and how difficult it is to find an academic position in this current job market. "But wait," he said, "aren't you already a professor?"

"No," I explained, "I basically do the work of a professor with the pay of a student." In retrospect, this was probably not the clearest answer that I could have given, but it was all I could think of at the moment.

But I realize that it isn't really his fault that he didn't know—so much of academia is steeped in mystery, even for those who are familiar with the inner workings of graduate school and beyond. For their part, my family members have had careers that are easy to recognize as "real work." My father never went to college, but he can fix anything. He worked as a mechanic for 47 years before he retired; my mother was a homemaker when I was little and worked in a nursery school when I got older. I still remember when she went to the local community college to get her certificate. This memory stands out to me because at age 12 or so, I was proofreading and editing her papers, instead of the other way around. It didn't seem unnatural to me then; I was lucky to be an avid reader and gifted writer at a young age and I was happy to share those talents with my mom.

It wasn't until much later that I realized how unusual this situation was—when my college friends recounted the ways in which their parents paid for extra tutoring or coached them through writing their personal essays on their college applications and still took the time to read their college papers. Meanwhile, with each break, I went home to discover that I had begun the gradual process of fundamentally *changing*—morphing into some new creature whom my family still loved but could not completely understand. It was as though I had suddenly started speaking a new language at home, but my voice still sounded the same to me.

And yet, I loved everything about being in college. I loved reading challenging, new texts that expanded my view of the world and having lively class discussions. I loved my English classes, in particular, and felt a deep sense of affection for my professors who found a way to make these classes accessible to a range of learners. In short, I wanted to be that person in a student's life, and I became determined to go to graduate school to earn my Ph.D. in English so that I, too, could one day open new doors for a future generation of students.

Four years later, I learned that applying to graduate school is unbelievably expensive for a person from a working-class background. Between applying for application fee waivers and working a paid research gig over winter break, I was able to scrounge together enough funding to pay for the chance to be considered as a graduate school candidate. But this was only the first of many unspoken truths about academia that I would soon learn.

I was fortunate to be accepted into a graduate program that offered tuition remission and a stipend. Although I could not afford to physically visit most of the places to which I applied, my current institution was within driving distance, so I excitedly scheduled a visit with the former chair and a tour of campus. In our email exchange, she asked if I wanted to meet with any of the faculty to discuss my research interests. Truth be told, I could not understand why they would want to meet with me then—I wasn't even a student there yet, and furthermore, I had no idea what my research interests would be. How would I even respond to that question? I thought the point of my M.A. was to figure out what my specialization would be. As such, I told her that wouldn't be necessary. Secretly, I thought, it would not be *worth* their time to meet with me.

I have found in my conversations with my fellow working class and first-generation students that we have a different concept of time; namely, that time is at least as valuable as money.

Arranging meetings with professors, seeking guidance, asking someone to read through a draft of a paper, all of these tasks meant that I would be "taking" some of their time, a debt that I did not know how to repay. So I reasoned it was better to not ask. I did not realize that my lack of meetings came off as a lack of commitment, until much later when my former Chair confided that she did not think I was interested in the department, and she was surprised when I accepted their offer.

By the time I began my graduate studies, I'd learned how to live comfortably enough on a modest budget. I learned how to make several variations of rice and pasta meals that sustained me from paycheck to paycheck. And most importantly, I learned how to ask for help from people who were more seasoned than I was. I finally accepted the fact that it was not an undue burden to ask for my professor's time.

When I finished my Master's degree, I decided not to participate in the graduation ceremony. The cost of renting the gown alone was enough to deter me, but more than that, I was waiting for my Ph.D. to enjoy the pomp and ceremony. My parents came down to visit with the intention of taking me out to lunch to celebrate in lieu of the ceremony. Instead, my car broke down on the way to the restaurant and we spent the afternoon on the side of the road waiting for AAA to respond and bring a new battery. When the technician finally arrived, my dad argued that the old battery was still good and could be saved. I realized that I come from a long line of people who were never too financially comfortable, never above saving something that could, maybe, potentially, one day be useful for something. Perhaps this sense of frugality is deeply embedded in my veins, given the amount of discarded draft fragments that I have saved on my computer, lest I want to use a turn of phrase again one day.

Now, nearly a decade later, I wonder what my parents must think of this time in my life. When their friends ask them what I do, my family tells them that I am a teacher. I actually love this response, because it dilutes my experiences down into an easily understood profession among working class folks, but more than that, it represents what I believe to be the best part of myself. I essentially went to graduate school to be a teacher. Granted, being a professor also entails doing a great deal of service work, research, writing, and hopefully publishing, but at my core, I *am* a teacher, and I like to think that is the trait that they most clearly see in me.

In my dissertation acknowledgements, I strive to honor those who prepared the way for me to have the privilege to be the first person with a Ph.D. in my family. As a student of literature, I believe in the power of storytelling and personal narratives. In my acknowledgements, I write:

> To my parents, I know that you might not think of yourselves as Writers (with a capital W), but every bedtime story, every conversation we had with my toys around the tea party table, and every time you encouraged my imagination led me to where I am now. I will always remember the time when I was in college and I was going through a particularly bad break up; you knew I loved getting

mail, so you sent me encouraging letters. Dad even included a draft of a short story he wrote about Jinx the squirrel. I still keep these mementos as reminders that during one of my darkest times, you gave me a gift that I have carried with me since then—a gift that I now strive to share with others. You gave me your words, and I thank you from the bottom of my heart.

Works Cited

Quarry, Justin. "Coming Out as Working Class." *CHE*, CHE, 22 July 2020, www.chronicle.com/article/coming-out-as-working-class/?cid2=gen_login_refresh.

Collaborative Writing for Publication in Undergraduate Literature Seminars

Ellen Scheible

In their 1990 article "Rhetoric in a New Key: Women and Collaboration," Andrea A. Lunsford and Lisa Ede describe collaborative writing as "a new rhetoric" that marks "a site of struggle, a site we see also as one of opportunity" (234). In this early piece, Lunsford and Ede chronicle their time exploring the status of collaborative writing in the university and the academy. Not surprisingly, their project leads them "to situate the issue of collaborative writing in a much broader historical, political, and ideological context and to contemplate the ways in which our society locates power, authority, authenticity, and property in an autonomous masculine self" (234). Lunsford and Ede's reference to the "autonomous masculine self" is also a coded way of describing the power dynamic that influences readers of tenure portfolios or book manuscripts and produces the voices in literary studies that decide an academic's fate, often tainting the view of an editor who is considering a collaboratively-produced piece of writing for publication. While it has been roughly 30 years since Lundsford and Ede's article emerged and their now mainstream, canonical work on collaborative writing began, the status of collaborative research and writing production in the Humanities, particularly in English departments and literature classrooms, is still uncertain. The silo effect of literary writing often takes precedence over more communal acts as faculty work to accomplish their research agendas and succeed within their fields. While still an assistant professor, I became interested in how the process of writing collaboratively could strengthen both the joy I get from writing in my discipline and the way I use that joy to teach my students the importance of writing and communication. This led me to consider collaborative writing as a pedagogical tool.

Alongside many of my colleagues in the field of literary studies, I have consistently been interested in why undergraduate research projects in the Humanities function differently from projects in almost every other discipline in the way that they value collaboration. Consequently, I put together a course on collaborative writing and publication in literature, which grew out of a workshop hosted by the office of Teaching and Learning at Bridgewater State University, where I teach in the English Department. At this workshop, I was asked to reflect on my role as a mentor for students in undergraduate research. I began thinking about my new course by asking rhetorically if it is even possible for Humanities faculty members, specifically those in literature, to collaborate with students on the writing of a critical essay with the goal of publication in a peer reviewed journal. I don't mean to spoil the ending, but the answer is yes and no.

After hearing about my course, the Director of Undergraduate Research asked me to participate in a panel presentation during the annual faculty research symposium that occurs on my campus. The panel was focused specifically on collaboration within undergraduate research and included mentors from different disciplines, but I was the only Humanities faculty member in the room, let alone on the panel. Even though I eagerly agreed to be a panel presenter, I realized during my preparation for the presentation that I really had not figured out how to collaborate with students in a way that would lead to, first, an effective articulation of threshold concepts in critical literary writing and, second, a real-life experience with the publication process, both of which were themes I volunteered to discuss on our panel. Further, I realized that the English department at my school, and most likely English departments at other state institutions like mine, continue to struggle with effective learning outcomes for our capstone courses. Thus, my presentation on the panel was more of an explanation of what we do *not* do as Humanities faculty members rather than an example of successful collaboration. After that panel discussion, it was clear that to figure out if writing and publishing with students in groups can really happen, I needed to create a capstone course where students could both articulate and emulate the creation and publication of a critical essay while collaborating with other students and a faculty member.

My approach in this new course that I titled "Writing and Literature" was to engage students as "partners," a term that has recently emerged in the scholarship of teaching and learning to address the way we decentralize authority in the classroom and position students to see themselves as peers in the larger discourse of academic scholarship.[1] During the spring semester of 2016, I taught my course for the first and, as of now, the last time. It was a senior seminar focused on the collaborative production of a 20-page critical essay. Our senior seminars cap at 15 students, and my goal was to give each student the experience of writing an essay collaboratively with heavy peer review and a focused workshop experience. I also wanted students to see the end goal as publication in a peer-reviewed journal, which led me to assign Wendy Laura Belcher's *Writing your Journal Article in 12 Weeks* as a text that would help pace our production. My in-class approach involved breaking the students into groups for the first part of the semester, and asking them to write an individual essay on one of three works of Irish fiction: a short story from James Joyce's *Dubliners*, Paul Murray's *Skippy Dies*, or Emma Donoghue's *Room*. They then produced short collaborative essays that we brought together later in the semester into a larger essay on each literary text. I wanted each work of fiction to speak together under similar themes that could unite them in the final essays. Ideally, as an Irish studies scholar, I wanted to send the essays to an Irish studies journal, such as *New Hibernia Review* or the *Irish University Review*, and ask the editors to publish them together as a new take on scholarly writing titled something like "collaborating with students on critical publishing."

During this process, I learned specific strategies that we, as faculty, can employ in such class experiences that are useful in developing and sustaining student/teacher partnerships in the Humanities. One strategy I employed was to model critical thinking, writing, and revision for our students in a hands-on way that students do not normally get to experience. We worked together through a published essay of mine so that I could emphasize my own revision process based on reader reviews and speak to how I built my argument, broke it down, and rebuilt it during the "revise and resubmit" phase of my submission. The goal was not necessarily for students to be able to write publishable essays as soon as they finished the course, but rather to be able to successfully articulate the components of healthy essay construction and, almost more importantly, to see revision as a type of collaboration. In an ideal world, collaborative writing would then be the foundation for the formation of firm writing skills with the idea that students might

---

1. See Cook-Sather et al.

see teambuilding and collaboration as fundamental to productive critical thinking and academic "silos" as less restrictive.

In terms of evaluation, I used oral interviews with students, self-assessment, and peer-assessment to evaluate student work, as well as a reflective essay about the process of essay creation. I also wanted the students to produce an exit portfolio of different versions of the essay that they turn in at the end of the semester—a process binder—where they can use the evaluation essay as a place to articulate what they "do" as English majors. Ideally, this would be the tangible version of a capstone experience. This worked well for the students as they reflected on their course experience at the end of the semester. They also wrote brief reader reviews of the secondary essays that then functioned as part of the literature review for the introduction of their collaborative essay.

There were definitely challenges along the way during this course. One major challenge was what seems to be an underlying bias against producing and publishing collaborative work, especially with students, in the field of literary studies. This is, of course, not new to faculty in the Humanities, especially those in writing studies who are familiar with Lundsford and Ede's ongoing work in collaborative writing. As we all know, collaborating when writing in literary fields, as opposed to the fields of rhetoric and composition, is still highly unusual and not always respected. However, following Lundsford and Ede's lead, the current methodology employed by most Teaching and Learning centers at universities, rather than discipline-specific fields, encourages more collaboration in the Humanities with the end goal of encouraging process-based thinking for both students and faculty. I decided to use my course as an experimental medium for ways that I might forge ahead with collaboration in my own work as a literary scholar while also paying attention to the moments when it simply does not work for our discipline.

Ultimately, it did not work for me to collaborate with the students as a peer writer. In many ways, this can be attributed to what Joanne Larson, Stephanie Webster, and Mindy Hopper refer to as my unavoidable role of "gatekeeper" in a literature classroom where there is a focus on specific content. In "Community Coauthoring: Whose Voice Remains?," Larson, Webster, and Hopper found that the role of "gatekeeper" that many teachers are forced into by predesigned curriculum can "limit other participants' access to powerful discourses" and perpetuate "inequality" (148). I had hoped that I could work as a member in each of their groups, offering writing assistance and contributing to the production of knowledge, but my knowledge and experience, as well as the power dynamic created by my role as professor, made that an impossibility. So, students worked together in their own groups while I offered feedback and support. In this way, I was not able to dismantle the unequal balance between teacher and learner during the semester in the way I had hoped. We were also challenged by the newness of the simple activity of partnering. Student partnerships become formulations of technology where pedagogy is exposed at its basic level, and this can feel uncomfortable and off balance at times. Managing that balance and recognizing that collaboration does not always result in equal amounts of production for every student created a new way of thinking for both me and the students. The greatest challenge we faced came at the end of the semester when we realized that the essays simply were not publishable. It was idealistic to imagine that we'd produce collaborative, publishable essays by undergraduate students in just a semester, but I really did think it was possible (and still do). In the next configuration of this class I want to figure out how to reach that goal.

Through this experience I gained numerous insights about teaching, learning, education, collaboration, and partnership. I learned that I was correct: students better learned to write a successful critical essay when collaborating towards the goal of publication rather than only writing alone with the goal of a final grade. With enough motivation and time to revise departmental learning outcomes, this reflection could prove to be a solid foundation forward for revising capstone curriculum. I had hoped that writing with students across a semester might strengthen my own writing skills and increase my production of publishable work, but this did not happen for me. It did, however, happen for the students, some of whom continued to work on their essays towards the goal of publication. I definitely feel that I could move forward with a collaborative model for many of my future senior seminars. Inviting students to write together (instead of writing alone) helps to demystify the process of academic writing and encourages students to articulate what it is that they actually learn as literature majors in college. Student partnerships also push faculty members to think less didactically about our roles in classrooms and more from the perspective of problem or project-based learning, while also offering a sense of belonging (Cook-Sather 3-11).

Emphasizing student responsibility is fundamental if we want to decentralize the authority in the classroom in the way that Paulo Freire famously emphasizes in "The Banking Concept of Education," an essay that underscores all aspects of my pedagogy:

> The pursuit of full humanity . . . cannot be carried out in isolation or individualism, but only in fellowship and solidarity, therefore it cannot unfold in the antagonistic relations between oppressors and oppressed. No one can be authentically human while he prevents others from being so. (85)

Partnering with students on even a basic level—asking what books should be read, what assignments need revision, how a student might construct a syllabus or submit a piece for publication—does not usually result in a complete class overhaul. Instead, students develop pride in their membership in the classroom community. At my own university, our first-generation students struggle fundamentally with building community in the classroom and building trust with their faculty leaders and peer reviewers. Student partnerships, both as models and as a direct experience, can help our students to build that trust in a more efficient and timely manner and to come together as community members in nontraditional but highly productive ways.

Works Cited

Belcher, Wendy Laura. *Writing Your Journal Article in 12 Weeks: A Guide to Academic Publishing Success.* Sage Publications, 2009.

Cook-Sather, Alison and Peter Felten. "Where Student Engagement Meets Faculty Development: How Student-Faculty Pedagogical Partnership Fosters a Sense of Belonging." *Student Engagement in Higher Education Journal*, vol.1, no. 2, 2017, pp. 3-11.

Cook-Sather, Alison, Catherine Bovill, and Peter Felten. *Engaging Students as Partners in Learning & Teaching: A Guide for Faculty.* Jossey-Bass, 2014.

Freire, Paulo. *Pedagogy of the Oppressed: 30th Anniversary Edition*. Trans. Myra Bergman Ramos. Continuum, 2005.
Larson, Joanne, Stephanie Webster, and Mindy Hopper. "Community Coauthoring: Whose Voice Remains?" *Anthropology & Education Quarterly*, vol. 42, no. 2, 2011, pp. 134-53.
Lunsford, Andrea A. and Lisa Ede. "Rhetoric in a New Key: Women and Collaboration," *Rhetoric Review*, vol. 8, no. 2, 1990, pp. 234-241.

(Emily 479)

Because I could not stop to Cite –
The Teacher did stop me –
She said this would be in my File –
For all Eternity.

She slowly spoke of Consequences
And I'd have given up that day
My sports and my leisure too,
To make It go away –

We learned at School, where Children write
To always name Sources –
But I was in a hurry then –
To pass all those Courses –

But she would not pass me –
And Summer suddenly grew chill –
For only Summer School, my Days –
Homework nights – no frills –

—Naomi Gades

tra/versing the year

(words like seeds dropping
through seasons of poetry
from the leaves of books)

rough winds tousle May
buds muscle open in an
agony of green

summer is cumin
spiced air hovering like bees –
sweet and stinging heat

night
    and
  leaves
        falling
clouds slide across tree-sliced moon –
goldengrove grieving

silent icicles
dripping slippery from eaves
in frozen sunlight

—Paul M. Puccio

BOOK REVIEWS

Inserting Oneself in the Story: Queer Literacy, Comics, and an Admonition to Move

Irene Papoulis

The books reviewed in this issue are on disparate topics. The reviewers, too, are very different people, with distinct vantage points: a rhetorician, a compositionist, and a retired bilingual elementary school teacher. Nevertheless, a connecting thread here is the way each reviewer weaves themself into their readings of the books. Marino recognizes himself as a version of the "queer literate" that Mark McBeth defines; in his review, we learn some of the story of Marino's own curation, growing up, of a queer archive of "ephemera." Romatz describes her experience being inspired at a presentation by the writers of the two books she went on to review, Emil Ferris and Nick Sousanis, who described how drawing fueled their thinking and writing. Romatz realized that the theories of freewriting and other composition strategies at the root of her own teaching of writing could be applied to comics and drawing. She resolved to find ways to explore the implications of the visual more deeply, perhaps at a future AEPL conference. In a sense she is following Twyla Tharp's prescription as H. Papoulis describes it in her review: to keep moving and growing in new directions. As Papoulis reflected on her personal experience of the resentments generated in her by difficult administrators and life circumstances, she too developed a personal engagement with Tharp's advice. All in all, these books and these reviewers, with their emphasis on expansive notions of texts, processes, and ways of being—to include artistic orientation, visuality, corporeality and movement, materiality and artifacts, as well as a range of personal and professional experiences and perspectives—embody the distinctive spirit that animates AEPL and this journal.

✦

McBeth, Mark. *Queer Literacies: Discourses and Discontents*, **Lexington Books, 2019, 280 pages.**

Nicholas Marino
Trinity College

Reading Mark McBeth's *Queer Literacies: Discourses and Discontents* brought me on a personal journey through my own literacy development as a queer individual. In addition, the book offers a useful theoretical framework and methodology for studying, researching, and writing about queer literacy. In the review that follows, I first present a recap of this framework and its scholarly contribution; then, I conclude with my personal connection to the text.

To begin, McBeth's book is aptly titled given the scope and methods of his project. From the start, his intentions are clear: he will not only unite and extend the imbricated discourses of literacy, identity, and sexuality, but also do so in purposeful opposition to mainstream, heteronormative discourses that control and suppress such knowledges. And yet, despite this almost adversarial approach, McBeth never stoops to defensiveness, but instead cultivates his "discontent" with heternormative-homophobic literacy sponsors—whether they are institutions like schools and libraries or entrenched academic concepts—into a pleasurably defiant project that positions queer voices at the center of literacy scholarship. The result is a new personal-political method to investigating, writing about, and working with archival materials; he coins it a "narrative-cum-analytic" approach that "demonstrates how paraphernalia and archival documents conjoined with memoir and critical analysis can combine into critical experimental genres" (25). This methodology—which fuses archival work, auto-ethnography, and high theory—aids McBeth as he reflects upon and builds a rhetorical framework around personal ephemera (i.e. school work, drawings, papers, etc.) from his educational history. Against this literacy background, he also maps out his own process of coming out, exploring the literacy journeys he undertook to understand and define his queerness through a paucity of print resources that sketched homosexuality in terms of perversion, not pleasure, and abjection, not identity. In doing so, McBeth pushes against the personal and scholarly discontents with heteronormative and homophobic discourses, which use "strategies of debasement and silence ... to reproduce and control a normative sexual worldview" (31).

This resistance generates a new subject position, that of the queer literate, who carves out their own literacy subversively and in direct contradistinction to the normative ideological freights imparted by literacy sponsors. At its core, *Queer Literacies* builds off Deborah Brandt's foundational work in "Sponsors of Literacy," while also integrating the pioneering work of literacy scholars highlighting queer and minority experiences. To name a few notable examples: Ellen Louise Hart ("Literacy and the Lesbian/Gay Learner"), Eric Darnell Pritchard (*Fashioning Lives: Black Queers and the Politics of Literacy*), Jaqueline Jones Royster (*Traces of a Stream: Literacy and Social Change Among African American Women*), Jonathan Alexander (*Literacy, Sexuality, Pedagogy*), and José Esteban Muñoz (*Cruising Utopia*). Uniting each of these projects through his own work, McBeth demonstrates that the queer literate is not an aberration, but actually produced by the process of literacy sponsorship itself. As McBeth states, "If these heteronormativizing literacy forces have sustained their dominant positions through an ongoing front of rhetorical-literate strategies, Queers would over the span of the twentieth century also labor to read the sources that oppressed them, research knowledge and worlds that others refused to acknowledge, and write new narratives that revised antagonistic readings of homosexuality" (32). Thus, queer literates emerge from their personal rejection of and resistance to the heternormative-homophobic discourses embedded within their sponsors' literacy training. Alone, the queer literate may seem sadly lost, an individual pitted against mainstream forces of suppression. However, when one's story is placed in the context of other queer literates, what emerges is a community of subjects, with a complex, rich history, struggling against and remaking literacy platforms in their image.

McBeth's narrative-cum-analysis approach is a successful tool for uncovering and combining these shared struggles and resistances. Of note, in Chapter 2, "Archival Tracks and Traces," he explores the memoir genre to reveal how queers, in their early stages of identity development, seek out literature about homosexuality, only to find that their identities are shrouded in the language of perversion. Even more, some accounts mention how literacy sponsors such as libraries, schools, and bookstores kept the books in literal and figurative jail, locked away from the general public and only available by request. The watchful eyes of the librarians and other patrons served to regulate and withhold such literacy, thereby reinforcing the sponsored view of homosexuality as abnormality. In Chapter 5, "Gay book? Libraries? That rang bells for me!," McBeth investigates how various activist movements within the American Library Association (ALA) attempted in the years after the Stonewall Riots to remedy this situation by "upending the tsk-tsk of heternormative biblio-techniques and replace it with literate sponsorships in which Queer literates could find accurate facts and empowering words to buoy themselves" (133). In tracking the Gay Task Force's work within the ALA, we witness how important inroads were made to provide access to reputable resources, while at the same time others criticized ALA's lack of support for queer people within the library system itself. Thus, the narrative-cum-analysis in this chapter illustrates the complexity of sponsors, who are not simply unified figure-heads, but stratified organizations with multiple valences of power often at odds within itself. The throughline between Chapter 2 and Chapter 5, which covers the personal experiences of the sponsored and the institutional perspective of the sponsor, seems to suggest that McBeth is only interested in traditional literacy platforms (i.e. libraries, schools, etc.). However, Chapter 6, "Psycho-Babble" and Chapter 7, "Viral Impetus" explore how literacy in specialized fields, like psychology and the medical community, filter down into the cultural zeitgeist shaping general knowledge. Each case study is composed of the voices and perspectives of individual queer literates, quilted together in the chapter and across the book, creating the impression of a powerful, unifying experience that these individuals have suffered through, challenged, and still continue to overcome.

Given that *Queer Literacies* puts the author's own voice and experience into conversation with memoirists, activists, and critical theorists, it's appropriate then that I interject my own narrative into this review of the project. In particular, I want to reflect upon the implicit connection McBeth makes between queerness, collecting, and coming of age. While he doesn't explicitly reflect on this relationship, it is embedded within his inspiration for the book. For instance, when cleaning out his family home after his mother's passing, McBeth came across an archive of schoolwork, projects, drawings, etc. that his mother saved and housed safely within a desk drawer. Pouring over these artifacts, he was transported mentally to the sites and contexts of literacy learning, while also seeing how various sponsors shaped his experience of growing up queer in conservative central Pennsylvania. I couldn't help but think of the various collections I amassed as a queer youth and the ways in which collecting is a queer literacy act. When I was young, my parents often called me a packrat and, for this reason, my grandmother always brought me trinkets from vacations, impromptu shopping trips, or catalogue buying sprees. "Nicholas loves his doodads," she would say to my mother at the kitchen table, which was just a little too big for the breakfast nook. I remember this explicitly because part of the table was jammed next to the counter, creating a private lean-to where I'd play with my trinkets until they were chipped or threadbare. Once the novelty wore off, doodads were never tossed out. Instead, they lived in another sacred space, the tiny drawer next to my nightstand.

A queer archive in its own right; I can still picture it in my mind's eye. Immediately, I see a half-melted ballerina candle from my little cousin's birthday cake. I took it because it was pretty, and I hid it deep within the drawer so no one would find it. Its charred tip would brush against other items leaving traces of its history. For instance, I can actually remember tracing my finger over the charcoal smudges on "subscription" tickets for bodybuilding magazines, which I pulled from glossy pages while my mother finished shopping in the supermarket. There were pages and pages of superhero drawings and cassette tapes of recording artists that my friends and older brother thought were too girly to listen to. Each artifact stands out to me as the crystallization of a particular learning experience, as I transformed into a queer literate. More specifically, each doodad became a vehicle for gender play, as off-brand G.I. Joe's did splits, ballet, and partnered off with other male toys and figures. The more precious of the doodads, which I wouldn't dare put in the drawer with the abrasive wick of the ballerina candle, occupied a shelf in my mother's curio cabinet. This collection provided a chance to learn the art of domestic work, as I played at dusting, cleaning, and arranging these items for display. Then, in the more traditional sense, I sharpened my reading prowess with bodybuilding magazine advertisements. My physical education class involved secretly dancing to female pop-songs of the late 80s and early 90s. Like McBeth, I can also see those who sponsored that literacy: my grandmother who gave a fresh supply of trinkets with every visit, my friends and brother who pushed my musical inclinations underground, the abstract and distant publishers of bodybuilding magazines and comic books who boosted my imagination.

Until reading *Queer Literacies*, I thought I was alone in my curation of vast collections of ephemera that appealed to a secret, subversive side of myself that I couldn't quite grasp yet. "Why do you want to keep *that*?" friends and family would ask. I could never quite articulate why. Without a compelling reason to defend this collection, the queer archive in my bedside drawer was thrown out, then slowly replaced, then dumped, and built up again several times. The shedding of so many skins in my growth as a queer literate. The focus on archiving that spurs McBeth's book raises for me new connections to material rhetorics and social literacies, as well as the post-human impact of literacy learning. There're still a few boxes of ephemera in the eaves of my parents' house, begrudgingly saved when I became empowered enough to say I wanted to keep them. Long after I'm gone, these artifacts will speak for me: what will they say to my niece and nephew and their children about who their uncle was at different ages of his life? What will they reveal about social and cultural materials that shaped my growth into a literate, confident, gay man? What unknown cost was there in throwing away all of those past literacy materials? What would I give to hold, reflect upon, and write about the contents of that drawer again? *Queer Literacies* attests to the fact that every queer individual should hang onto, reflect upon, and chart their own archive of literacy growth, even if the reasons for doing so aren't clear. By sharing the contents of that secret drawer with others, we will find, in retrospect, a collective testament of our survival against literacy sponsors who told us that our self-knowledge wasn't valid, that we shouldn't exist, and that we can't be proud of the queer literates we've become.

Ferris, Emil. *My Favorite Thing Is Monsters*, Fantagraphics, 2017, 416 pages.
Sousanis, Nick. *Unflattening*, Harvard UP, 2015, 208 pages.

Wilma Romatz

C. S. Mott Community College, retired

In February 2020, just before the Covid curtains came crashing down on our world, an invitation to the Michigan State University Comic Forum piqued my attention. The Forum was to feature two speakers, Emil Ferris, the author of an award-winning graphic novel, *My Favorite Thing is Monsters*, and Nick Sousanis, the award-winning author of *Unflattening*, which was written and drawn in comic format as his dissertation at Columbia. According to the forum flyer, Sousanis's book "argues for the importance of visual thinking in teaching and learning." That description was too enticing to ignore since I had finished my own dissertation about visual thinking through the English Department at MSU in 2002, studying the ways drawing could affect my community college composition students' writing. I learned later that several of the early pages of *Monsters* were Ferris's thesis for her Masters in Creative Writing at the School of the Art Institute of Chicago.

Both books have been around long enough to spark considerable response, but they remain important through the interviews, websites, and lectures that have brought Sousanis and Ferris's work to a wide audience. It is exciting to know that sequels to both books are in the works.

Sousanis's wide-ranging research that she presented that Saturday in February was as exciting as I had hoped it would be, but I was surprised to find myself equally drawn to Ferris's presentation. Even though on the surface, Ferris's world of monsters and horror comics is so different from Sousanis's world, the two works share several major themes. *Monsters* is drawn in a variety of graphic techniques from loose to highly rendered cross-hatching, both black and white and in color. *Unflattening*'s more academic approach strives to embody the theory behind visual thinking with precise and measured complex drawings. Both creators are very passionate about their work—a prerequisite for the depth and width of the two books. That passion led me to purchase both books, and now I am passionate about them too.

The theorists Sousanis cites—among others, Rudolph Arnheim, Suzanne K. Langer, Lev Vygotsky, and especially Maxine Greene—were familiar to me from my research, and perhaps their voices resonate among *JAEPL* readers as well. However, it is the way in which Sousanis develops and presents these theories that makes the book inspirational. He weaves and spins ideas from ancient Greece to modern times in words and images together. Graphic memoirs and novels were already popular when he began in 2004, but drawing a dissertation was a totally new venture. The idea didn't emerge full-grown for him either. For his first class at Columbia with Maxine Greene in the early 2000s, he drew his response for her class, describing her as a spinning top—a metaphor he developed in several other comics—and that gave him the idea to go even larger with the process.

Unflattening

The opening lines and images of *Unflattening* present a powerful graphic illustration of what Sousanis sees as the condition of today's world. He writes, "Like a great weight, descending, suffocating, and ossifying, flatness permeates the landscape." These words march through fifteen pages of drawings of mummy-like figures moving along on rolling sidewalks, heads looking down, heading for a huge education factory where they will be adjusted and molded. Sousanis shows how "our vision has been shuttered… boxed into bubbles of our own making" (14), leaving us with narrow vision, unable to see beyond our own boundaries of thought. His image of human development through history is a page of beautiful spinning tops, "darting, dancing, animated and teeming with possibilities," that have now fallen over and their energy has been "curtailed, never set in motion, leaving only flatness" (16-17).

He compares these figures to Edwin Abbott's two-dimensional inhabitants of *Flatland* (originally published in 1882) who can see nothing beyond their flat plane of existence. Sousanis's prescription for what we must do to escape this flatness is to develop double vision. He points out that because our eyes see stereoscopically, by integrating two views we can perceive depth. In the same way, "Unflattening is a simultaneous engagement of multiple vantage points from which to engender new ways of seeing" (32). He will develop this metaphor through the rest of the book to make the point that seeing with "double vision" lets us escape being stuck in a rut, guided like puppets on strings because of our culture, background, and training. It makes it possible for us to become willing to see others' viewpoints and to work to bridge the gaps between groups and individuals.

The shape of our thoughts, Sousanis contends, is limited by the languages we use for thinking. In panels and whole-page illustrations he depicts the way that drawings (here in comic format) can move back and forth between the linear—words marching across the page and the "all-at-onceness" of the image—to better represent what actually happens when one thinks (58). He cites several experts who have researched the differences between *sequential* and *simultaneous* kinds of awareness, illustrating each in a medium that moves back and forth between both modes. "Words…are not the sole vehicle for communicating thought…[and] comics, beyond uniting text and image, allow for the integration and incorporation of multiple modes and signs and symbols" (65). For him, however, make no mistake—images are not mere illustrations of the words, but together they communicate more than either words or images can say alone. He says, "Drawing *is* my thinking" (Keynote).

In addition to what we perceive visually, he explores the concept of how our bodies in motion, bodies as modes of thought, add another dimension to thought. The physical movement required to draw affects thought. He says, "drawing is a way of seeing and thus, a way of knowing, in which we touch more directly the perceptual and embodied processes underlying thinking" (78). When we draw "we thus extend our thinking—distributing it between conception and perception," engaging both simultaneously. "We draw not to transcribe ideas from our heads but to generate them in search of greater understanding" (79). An elegantly curved full-page dancing figure shows how "Drawer and Drawing journey forth into the unknown together." His drawings make the theory come to life on the page. Although Sousanis doesn't mention Sondra Perl's "felt sense" or Peter Elbow's "embracing contraries," he appears to be influenced by these classic concepts from composition theory that Maxine Greene surely must have talked about with him.

The fullness of this book creates the potential for unlimited discussion of these vast and compelling topics, and he has so much work available on his website that anyone interested in digging into both the theory and its practical application has a rich field to explore. Throughout the reading I kept wanting to see Sousanis's process for constructing his drawings, and I was happy to find that the appendix includes several pages of the beginning drawings and brainstorming he used to work out the theory and layout for the book. In one interview he admitted that he had made at least fifty drawings to come up with one page. He only shows a bit of the process in the appendix, but it is a good start for understanding how his "drawing *is* his thinking," as he said in the forum and other lectures.

From the beginning of his work on his dissertation at Columbia, Sousanis published his progress in his blog. Now he generously has published his syllabi for his classes on thinking through comics along with exercises and examples of student work. The blog, *Spinweaveandcut.com* is an inspiring— and practical—source that could be instrumental in achieving some of the reform needed for today's virtual education problems, with the increasing emphasis on the visual.

Sousanis's lectures from several conferences and forums also have been posted on YouTube. In one he said, "Everything I do is to try to help people see themselves in a new light…[to ask] 'how can you look at something and see yourself and our environment in new ways?'" *Unflattening* has been published in seven languages, and Sousanis says he is amazed at the popularity of his work.

My Favorite Thing Is Monsters

Emil Ferris's presentation inspired me to explore just what it is that makes some people love horror. To tell the truth, I have never really been a fan of horror of any kind, and I probably would not have picked up the book without first hearing Ferris talk. The wide scope of her background and insight began to change my mind within the first few minutes. Ferris talked about how drawing had essentially saved her life after scoliosis kept her from walking until she was three. She felt like a monster much of her life. Then, after she contracted West Nile Virus at age forty and became paralyzed, drawing was her means for recovery. Not only does she show why she loves monsters, and why the monsters we have created need and deserve love, her book demonstrates the healing powers of making art.

This amazing 400 page, four pound novel, devoid of pagination, is only slightly disguised autobiography. Its format is the hand-drawn, hand-written journal of ten-year old Karen Reyes, filled with her account of growing up in the sixties in Chicago, feeling like a misfit. Using only ballpoint and Flair pens as a child might do, she is able to tell a compelling and complex story. In spite of the darkness of Karen's life and experiences, a sense of hope underlies even the most difficult parts of the story, and both large and small details offer an intriguing perspective on life with bits of surprise and humor along the way.

We meet Karen in her bedroom in the basement of a once elegant building in Chicago that she says "smells like the early Impressionism of Vincent Van Gogh—all big strokes of umber and ochre—a peppery greasy I love you smell." She dreams that she is in danger; she howls as a screaming mob comes down her street. She changes into a werewolf saying "it is easier being a monster than being a human girl." She maintains this werewolf persona that represents how she sees herself throughout the novel.

It is easy to love this small girl with fangs and an under bite whose depiction is reminiscent of Sendak's drawing in *Where the Wild Things Are* and who is set on understanding the wrongs she sees around her, as she tries to figure out how to live through the pain of growing up.

She soon learns that her beautiful upstairs neighbor Anka Silverberg is dead, found shot in the heart and tucked neatly in bed. The police ruled it a suicide, even though Anka had been shot in her living room. This makes no sense to Karen, so she borrows her older brother's hat and trench coat and becomes a detective. She explores hidden parts of her building and checks on the alibis of her strange neighbors.

Karen doesn't understand her older brother Deeze's many sexual relationships that he doesn't even attempt to hide from her, letting her see him in all his own brokenness. She loves him deeply and worries about him. He protects her and takes her to the Art Institute of Chicago, where she has an unusual relationship with the paintings she says are her "friends." Ferris has Karen draw several of her favorite paintings in her journal in great detail and also lets Deeze explain some of them to Karen, including their monster imagery. She says, "I remember Deeze laughed when I told him that the witch [in Saftleven's *A Witches' Sabbath*] smelled like wood smoke and egg salad sandwiches." Ferris thus gives the reader a new perspective on these works of art. Later Karen imagines herself being pulled into some of the more frightening paintings.

Early in the Comic Forum lecture, Ferris talked about the *vesica piscus*, sacred geometry, and Imoto's research on the effect of Tibetan priests' prayer on water. Intriguing as it was, at first that seemed to be a distraction in the middle of a discussion on her life, Mary Shelley's *Frankenstein*, and monsters. However, the symbolism of the *vesica piscus*, the almond shape formed in the center of two overlapping circles, is central to Ferris's composition throughout the book as Ferris pointed out in her lecture. Deeze explains to Karen that it is very ancient knowledge, and that "the pyramids, ancient temples, cathedrals and even the Art Institute were all designed using it." Everything is energy, Ferris said, and this symbol represents all the dichotomies—mother/father, above/below, life/death, and the transition from one world to another. There are certainly many dichotomies, triangles and almond shapes in this book.

The Chicago of *Monsters* was a complicated place to grow up in 1968 with the murder of Martin Luther King setting off rebellions and the poverty and danger of Karen's (and Ferris's) neighborhood. Ferris has drawn over fifty pages to show this setting and these monstrous events in great detail. Against this background, Karen is trying to come to terms with what love means, and with her own sexuality. She thinks about all the women who seem to be addicted to Deeze. She is assaulted one evening by classmates and punished by the nuns for defending herself, even though she is the victim.

In response she goes home and draws the cover of a Ghastly comic, a huge warty, claw-toothed head leering over a frightened man and woman. Above it she writes, "Love is actually the weirdest Monster out there."

Throughout her journal, Karen turns to drawing these covers as a way to deal with her fear and stress. When Karen learns that her mother is dying of cancer, a journal page shows her rage. Later, over the DREAD cover she writes "Dear notebook—I'll tell you straight—in my opinion the best horror magazine covers are the ones where the lady's boobs aren't spilling out as she's getting attacked by a monster. Those covers give me something worse than the creeps. I think the boob covers send a secret message that it is very dangerous to have breasts—and considering what Mama is going through, maybe the magazines know stuff that we don't...."

And yet there is humor in the depiction of this life. The hand-drawn monster-themed valentines Karen gives her classmates made me laugh out loud. One says, "I would have given you my heart but all I could spare was this ventricle," a piece of macaroni with red food coloring dripped over it like blood. She risks having the nuns confiscate her notebook but draws several monster cards on her math paper including a "shrieking violet" and a heart-shaped box filled with eyeballs. Karen is surprised that the nuns tell her she will go to hell for reading horror comics even after telling the class about the "'cephalophore' saints like St. Denis who carry their own heads." Deeze tells her that St. Christopher, "the 'Dog-headed' saint...[is his] main (wolf) man." A very Egyptian-looking, wolf-headed character tells Karen, "if I can be a saint, then you can definitely be a detective." Like the many references to Egyptian mythology, this wolf-head appears throughout the novel.

Several of the carefully rendered portraits look almost sculpted on the page. There is much heart and feeling in the way Ferris draws her characters and it is clear, as she said in an interview, that she *feels* the characters as she draws them. She said it's a family joke that her daughter comes in and asks, "Which character are you crying about this time?"

It is difficult to miss the symbolic significance in the fact that the murder victim Anka Silverberg represents life, and the difficulties she faced are significant on more than a personal level. Anka is always drawn in blue ink, wearing scarab earrings, and her cat whose forehead fur is in the shape of the *ankh* (the Egyptian symbol of life) is named King Tut. As an extensive flashback, in her detective role, Karen listens to Anka's recording of her difficult early life during the Holocaust and draws many pages of those images in her journal as she listens. The hatred of the mob reverberates throughout the story in stark contrast with the love shown by the prostitutes who took Anka in and raised her. It is easy to compare Anka's experiences in 1940's Germany with what was going on both in 1968 Chicago, and what is happening today. Karen says, "A Nazi is a person who chooses to NOT SEE anything that would keep them from being cruel...even if what they will NOT SEE is how their cruelty will destroy them."

The irony in this book, and what it borrows from horror comics and film, is the idea that the true "monsters" are good. They are the misunderstood, the misfits, the different. The villagers are the mob, the unthinking followers whom Karen identifies as the Mean, Ordinary, and Boring. "A good monster sometimes gives somebody a fright because they're weird looking and fangy...a fact that is beyond their control...but bad monsters are all about control...they want the whole world to be scared so that bad monsters can call the shots." Perhaps Nick Sousanis would say they are the Flatlanders. Perhaps they are related to 21st century politics.

For both Sousanis and Ferris, comics are one answer to the divides we are experiencing in today's society, a means for rising above the narrow constraints media, history, and culture have placed upon us. That comic art rather than "fine" art would be the medium they choose to express that position might seem far-fetched to some, but to others, it could not be more appropriate. Drawing comics is a metaphor for thinking beyond the fixed, "that's the way it's always been," a place where we don't think about any "side" but our own. When we begin to try to see the other side, (and realize that there are no sides) we stop being "Not-Sees."

Neither book is a quick read and delving into them has evoked a year-long explosion of thought and a shift in my own perception as well. Several times while reading, I have recalled themes from AEPL conferences I have attended, and I could envision featuring these two comic artists in a future gathering in the mountains.

Sousanis explores the theory behind drawing as thinking in carefully drawn page after page of deep intellectual compositions. Ferris' book is a *tour de force* and an example of the beauty of working in both words and images. As I read, it struck me that *Monsters* is a literary work on the scale of Nathaniel Hawthorne's allegorical novels, and at the same time, its art elevates the comic genre to a high level. Together they say if we keep thinking of writing in words alone, we miss so much of what is possible. For teachers, writers, and artists, the important thing is that literally putting pen to paper in whatever way one's skills allow opens the boundaries of thought to new and exciting directions.

Works Cited

Ferris, Emil. http://www.emilferris.com

—. Speaking as a distinguished alum at The School of the Art Institute of Chicago https://www.youtube.com/watch?v=JpgP2SJSqyQ

Jennings, Dana. "First, Emil Ferris Was Paralyzed. Then Her Book Got Lost at Sea." https://www.nytimes.com/2017/02/17/arts/design/first-emil-ferris-was-paralyzed-then-her-book-got-lost-at-sea.html.

Sousanis, Nick. https://spinweaveandcut.com/unflattening/

—. https://spinweaveandcut.com/maxine-eugene/

—. http://www.comicsforum.msu.edu/2020/02/22/2020-msu-comics-forum-keynote-address-livestreams-archived/

—. https://www.youtube.com/watch?v=c6cASACXOAQ Nick Sousanis speaking with Professor Latinx

✢

Tharp, Twyla. *Keep It Moving: Lessons for the Rest of Your Life.* Simon and Schuster, 2019, 190 pages.

Helen Papoulis

Are you dreaming about retirement? Are you already retired? This is the book for you!

Although it holds much wisdom applicable to people of all ages, it is especially pertinent for teachers in our older years. Tharp's beautiful book intertwines the wisdom from her long career as a world-renowned choreographer with inspiring stories about people from a variety of fields ranging from music to religion to boxing. Their stories emerge like a chorus of dancers in their common refusal to stagnate or give up. Teachers, in particular, could benefit from this book since we are often all too ready to deny our own power.

While reading, I imagine Tharp standing near me tapping her foot, begging me to open my eyes, look ahead, and go, go, go, with no holds barred. She urges the reader to "Be Daring," "Take a leap." She says, "The Time is Now" (111-12). She tells us to fly, take up space, and never to stagnate or to settle.

I was a Spanish bilingual public school teacher in San Francisco for years. I came to the job with a sense of joy and a deep love for the children, who appreciated my understanding of them and my child-centered approach to learning. I formed many partnerships with my students' families who felt welcome in the classroom and formed a close-knit community with them.

My retirement of eight years and the years leading up to it have taught me many important lessons. Nevertheless, I wish I had had the opportunity to read *Keep It Moving* ten years ago while I was teaching. I might have struggled less and accomplished more.

I used to think I would continue to teach kindergarten at least into my seventies. I did not imagine ever wanting to retire. I enjoyed giving my students a sense of safety, empowerment, and love of learning. I aimed to teach them how to respect everyone and resolve conflicts peacefully. My students and their families respected and admired me, and the fact that former students of mine would always run up to me and hug me when I walked down the hall reinforced my sense of success.

Then one fall a new principal arrived at our elementary school and thus began my long painful descent into what seemed like a dark hole. She seemed more interested in order and appearance than in the students' well-being. Due to her negativity, all my enthusiasm for teaching began to slowly dissolve. Because our styles of teaching did not exactly align with hers, this new principal decided she did not like me and some of my colleagues, and she became determined to get rid of us. She divided the teachers into two groups: those she wanted to keep and those she wanted to get rid of. Those of us in the latter group tended to be less mainstream, often older and more interested in the well-being of the whole student than in a spic-and-span, laminated classroom. Due to her negative evaluations, I landed in PAR (peer assistance and review). I got a "coach," worked with her and promptly passed after a stressful semester of close scrutiny.

A few years went by, and my principal appeared to have let up. I assumed I was out of the woods. Then, during another evaluation year, I was placed in PAR for a second time! I soon learned that the district had decided to make the process of passing PAR much more difficult. I was assigned another "coach." I had to provide extremely detailed lesson plans, and I was subjected to countless unannounced visits. I was never clear about what I was doing wrong, other than the fact that my classroom was untidy at times, and I didn't chastise my students—whose families often worked two jobs and had to take public transportation to school—when they arrived a few minutes late. In the middle of that process, I was diagnosed with breast cancer, and I underwent treatment throughout the PAR process.

The end of PAR involved going in front of a large panel to present my case, to determine whether or not I would be fired, which would have meant losing my pension. It was so humiliating! I still have nightmares related to that room, which seemed much more like a criminal courtroom than anything connected to education. Luckily, many of the families of my present and former students showed up outside the large hall with letters in support of me, and I did pass. Soon after that, though, burned out and exhausted at only 56 years old, I decided to retire early.

I started retirement feeling extremely drained from the endless evaluation and the degradation generated by the PAR process and my cancer treatment. I felt frozen, contracted and resentful, nothing at all like the joyful teacher I had been earlier. I did everything that Tharp urges us not to do. I was stuck in the old pain and sense of humiliation I felt because someone had deemed me less worthy than I knew I was. In her chapter "Bouncing Back," Tharp speaks of major setbacks in our lives. She says "The ultimate purpose of bouncing back is not to repay the world with your scorn. It is to launch yourself into a better position, a higher perch" (115). In retrospect, I realize I was stuck in scorn. I was constantly ruminating about the unfairness of my situation. How could it be that I had poured so much energy, hard work and caring into my students and yet be confronted by such a brutal attack on my sense of integrity?

Even greater than my scorn was my sense of self-doubt. I compared myself to a good friend who had become teacher of the year the same year I was in PAR. My friend was getting an A+ in teaching, and I had not just gotten a "C," I had come very close to an "F." In the chapter "Build a Second Act," Tharp continues to encourage us to move ahead into positivity and to leave debilitating negativity behind. She says, "All master adjusters learn to push their strengths and drop everything else: resentment, insecurity, doubt, and physical handicaps" (147).

Keep it Moving would have helped me during that harrowing time. For example, at the time I was an exercise avoider, and I would have greatly benefited from her words of wisdom to move. She says "Your body is your job. If you don't work for it, it will not work for you." She addresses exercise avoiders by saying "just imagine you are exercising, if you are not ready to start" (34). The book has very simple and practical movement exercises scattered throughout.

Despite feeling exhausted and burned out, retirement offered me a sense of possibility. That renewed energy lasted for about a year until my wife of 31 years at that time was diagnosed with lung cancer. All my retirement hopes were shaken, and I was back into survival mode. I would have benefited a lot from the chapter "The Swap," in which

Tharp discusses the concept of "gravitas" and how to create a sense of centered peace, regardless of the difficulties life throws at you.

Throughout these seven years of being a caregiver to my wife and the roller coaster of treatments and remissions, I have floundered quite a bit in my professional life. Before retirement, I completed a certificate program in interpretation and a few years ago I completed a year-long online course in written translation. However, other than occasional volunteer work and a short period of working for an interpretation agency, I have not worked in my new career, even though I have the capability to do so. Despite the emotional toll that being a caregiver entails, Tharp's book would have helped me work towards clearer professional and creative goals.

While facing the challenge of my wife's cancer, I wish I could have read the chapter "Better for the Mending." Twyla Tharp asks us whether we are more ashamed of trying or of not trying. She explains the importance of expanding rather than contracting when faced with adversity. She also expresses how to appreciate the small positive moments in our everyday lives. She suggests that we ask ourselves, "Can you turn this situation into an opportunity for you to improve?" (165).

If I had the opportunity to read this book eight years ago, I think I would have accomplished more. I would have spent less time worrying, watching TV, and feeling depressed about aging. Tharp encourages us to take a deep look at our habits, our sense of ourselves. She urges us to reinvent, redefine and expand ourselves. She wants us to look ahead with anticipation and move forward regardless of the amount of time we may have left.

After reading *Keep It Moving*, I see myself through fresh eyes. I feel empowered to expand, grow, reinvent myself, take up space, and leave behind my old patterns.

This is a book to read and reread. You will want to leave it on your coffee table. Any random page read aloud will please your guests and spark a stimulating conversation.

If you're moving toward retirement, I hope her vibrant words will fly you into an experience that far exceeds all your expectations.

Be prepared to dust off your guitar, grab your skates, open your paint box or put on your boxing gloves and forge ahead with every ounce of your energy. Enjoy your newly acquired confidence and excitement as Twyla shows you how to leap and spin towards a future filled with movement, expansiveness, and joy!

Contributors to JAEPL, Vol. 26

Christopher Basgier is Acting Director of University Writing at Auburn University, where he helps faculty integrate writing and high impact practices into courses and curricula and leads professional development experiences for writing center peer consultants. His scholarship focuses on WAC, writing program administration, threshold concepts, and rhetorical genre theory. He is also a Unitarian Universalist and practitioner of meditation and contemplative writing. (chris.basgier@auburn.edu)

Jessica Berg is a teacher at Franklin Central High School on the south side of Indianapolis. She's been in the classroom for going on five years, and she's worked alongside Dr. Pamela Hartman to study and discuss using the arts in ELA classrooms since her time at Ball State University. (jessica.berg@ftcsc.org)

Michael-John DePalma is associate professor of English and coordinator of professional writing and rhetoric at Baylor University. His research centers on religious rhetorics, transfer, and rhetorical education. His recent work has appeared in *College English*, *College Composition and Communication*, *Composition Studies*, *Rhetoric Review*, and various edited collections. With Jeffrey M. Ringer, he edited *Mapping Christian Rhetorics: Connecting Conversations, Charting New Territories* (2015). He is the author of *Sacred Rhetorical Education in 19th Century America: Austin Phelps at Andover Theological Seminary* (2020). (Michael-John_DePalma@baylor.edu)

Hannah Fulton works in Fishers, Indiana as the Director of Student Advancement at Sylvan Learning Center. She has a Bachelor's and Master's degree from Ball State University. The research she and the other authors have completed in arts and literacy has led to multiple national and international conference presentations and a published book chapter. (hannah.r.fulton@gmail.com)

Naomi C. Gades teaches college English in western Maryland. Her research, which has been recognized with the Fathman Young Scholars Prize from the T. S. Eliot Society, investigates the intersection of science and modernist poetry. She has contributed to *The Robert Frost Review*, *JMMLA*, and *The Imaginative Conservative*. When she has spare time, she enjoys outdoor activities, video games, and composing questionable poetry. (ngades@luc.edu)

Denise Goldman is an adjunct professor of writing and research at Long Island University in Brookville, NY. Her work has been presented at the Phish Studies Conference, and will be published in an upcoming book dedicated to this discipline. (Denise.Goldman@liu.edu)

Christopher Sean Harris is an associate professor of writing studies at California State University, Los Angeles, where he teaches professional and technical writing, writing pedagogy, and language study courses. His research interests include online writing instruction, marginalia in writing textbooks, graduate student writing, and project-based learning. During his free time, Harris enjoys outings with his daughter, endurance sports, and upcycling. (charris3@calstatela.edu)

Pamela Hartman is associate professor of English at Ball State University, where she teaches courses in secondary English education, young adult literature, and multicultural literature. Her research focuses on using the arts to teach literacy and on the intersection of class, gender, and literacy. (pmhartman@bsu.edu)

Sarah Heidebrink-Bruno is a Ph.D. candidate in the English Department at Lehigh University, where she will soon graduate with a specialization in post-1945 American literature, feminist studies, and social justice pedagogies. After graduation, she will join the faculty at the English Department at Albright College. Her dissertation, "'How Will you Grow?': Restorative Justice in Contemporary American Women's Literature and Beyond," demonstrates how contemporary, American women novelists move readers beyond a limited understanding of justice that is based solely in juridical processes, and toward creative visions of community-based justice, which reflect diverse feminists' understandings of restorative justice practices. She lives in Bethlehem, PA with her spouse, her child, and her cat. (seb211@lehigh.edu)

Nicholas P. Marino is currently a lecturer in the Allan K. Smith Center for Writing and Rhetoric at Trinity College in Hartford CT. He received his PhD in English with a specialization in Rhetoric and Writing Studies from Purdue University in 2017. His research interests include multimodal composing, queer rhetorics, and masculinity studies. (nicholas.marino@trincoll.edu)

Helen Papoulis retired from her position as a Spanish Bilingual Elementary teacher with the San Francisco Unified School District in 2012. She now works as a translator, interpreter and acupuncturist. (helenpapoulis@gmail.com)

Paul M. Puccio is Professor of English at Bloomfield College, where he teaches all of the poems echoed in "tra/versing the year." He has published articles on contemplative teaching practices, Victorian schoolboys, 19th- and 20th-century British literature, music drama, and ghosts in CCC Online, Writing on the Edge, Dialogue, JAEPL, Reading Stephen Sondheim, The Encyclopedia of Catholic Literature, and Modern Language Studies. (paul_puccio@bloomfield.edu)

Jorge Ribeiro is an adjunct professor in the English Department at California State University, Los Angeles. He majored in religion as an undergraduate and spent 13 years in Japan, and during that time he was able to sit in zazen meditation at Eiheiji Temple for a week. His goal is to bring mindfulness into the classroom.

Wilma Romatz has combined her love for art and writing since childhood, earning double majors in studio art and English in undergrad in her home state of Kentucky, and ultimately completing a PhD dissertation at Michigan State University focusing on the effects of students' drawings on their writing in her community college composition classes. The research was heavily influenced by the 1995 AEPL conference keynotes of James Moffett and she has presented her research at subsequent AEPL conferences and many others, including an international conference in Bordeaux, France. Since retirement from Mott Community College in 2002 where her combined art/writing background was invaluable in her Children's Literature and composition classes, she has focused on her own writing and art, particularly printmaking, computer art, handmade books. She has exhibited in several galleries. (whromatz@gmail.com)

Kevin Roozen is a Professor of Writing and Rhetoric at the University of Central Florida. His research argues for semiotically richer and more fully dialogic perspectives of how literate persons and their textual practices come to be across moments and lives. In addition to *Expanding Literate Landscapes* (2017), Kevin's book with Joe Erickson, Kevin's scholarship has appeared in journals including *Written Communication* and *College Composition and Communication* and in a number of edited collections. (Kevin.Roozen@ucf.edu)

Ellen Scheible is Professor of English and Coordinator of Irish Studies at Bridgewater State University. She is author of "Imperialism, Aesthetics, and Gothic Confrontation in The Picture of Dorian Gray" in the Norton Critical Edition of *The Picture of Dorian Gray* (2020) and co-editor, with Claire Culleton, of *Rethinking Joyce's Dubliners* (Palgrave 2017). Her current projects include *Nation, Home and Body in Irish Fiction and Film*, a book project on the Irish domestic interior in modern and contemporary Irish literature, and *The Dark: A Critical Edition*, a coedited critical edition of John McGahern's novel. She has articles forthcoming on Edmund Burke and the body of the sublime, Irish domestic fiction, the Irish gothic, and the Irish bildungsroman. (ESCHEIBLE@bridgew.edu)

Brandon Schuler is a former secondary ELA teacher. He completed his Bachelor's in Secondary English Education at Ball State University and his Master's in Curriculum and Instruction at Purdue University. His research areas include integrating multicultural, young adult literature in the classroom and implementing the arts in literacy instruction. He has presented this research at multiple national and international conferences. (beschuler11@gmail.com)

JOURNAL OF TEACHING WRITING

IUPUI

SCHOOL OF LIBERAL ARTS
Indiana University
Indianapolis

The *Journal of Teaching Writing* (*JTW*) is a journal devoted to the teaching of writing at all academic levels and in any subject area. Our mission is to publish refereed articles and reviews that address the practices and theories that bear on our knowledge of how people learn and communicate through writing. Topics include writing and literacy, composition theory, revision, responding to writing, assessment, diversity in writing, information literacy, and others. An important part of our mission is demystifying the editorial review process for our contributors and modeling the teaching of writing as a process of reflection and revision. Submissions and subscription requests may be sent to our editorial assistant via email at jtw@iupui.edu.

PARLOR PRESS
EQUIPMENT FOR LIVING

New Releases

English Studies Online: Programs, Practices, Possibilities, edited by William P. Banks and Susan Spangler

Feminist Circulations: Rhetorical Explorations across Space and Time, edited by Jessica Enoch, Danielle Griffin and Karen Nelson.

Pedagogical Perspectives on Cognition and Writing, edited by J. Michael Rifenburg, Patricia Portanova, and Duane Roen

The Art of Public Writing by Zachary Michael Jack

MLA Mina Shaughnessy Prize and CCCC Best Book Award 2021!

Creole Composition: Academic Writing and Rhetoric in the Anglophone Caribbean, edited by Vivette Milson-Whyte, Raymond Oenbring, and Brianne Jaquette

Check Out Our New Website!

Discounts, blog, open access titles, instant downloads, and more.

And new series:

Comics and Graphic Narratives
Series Editors: Sergio Figueiredo, Jason Helms, and Anastasia Salter

Inkshed: Writing Studies in Canada
Series Editors: Heather Graves and Roger Graves

www.parlorpress.com

JAEPL **Discount:** Use JAEPL20 at checkout to receive a 20% discount on all titles not on sale through September 1, 2021.

www.ingramcontent.com/pod-product-compliance
Lightning Source LLC
Chambersburg PA
CBHW031335160426
43196CB00007B/692